W9-AOY-762

A Concise History of MUSIC

From Primitive Times
to the Present

by PERCY M. YOUNG

DAVID WHITE COMPANY
NEW YORK

Published in the United States of America by
David White, Inc.
60 East 55th Street
New York, NY 10022

Library of Congress Catalog Card Number : 72-83990
ISBN *87250-455-x*
Printed in Great Britain

TITLE PAGE: Trumpet duet with cymbals
from a 13th century Psalter

Preface

MUSIC IS A PART of nature. Music is sound – and sound emerges from all the creatures of the earth, small and large, as well as from the elements in our environment. There are soft, flowing, gentle sounds; and harsh, strident, violent sounds. There are sounds that soothe us, or stimulate us to needed action, or provoke us to hostile acts. And they are all around us, as they were all around our ancestors many thousands of years ago.

Just as music is a part of nature, so each one of us is a part of nature. It is not surprising, therefore, that we are greatly affected by music. It is, in fact, hardly possible for us to escape it. Music is a pleasure to many, but it is also a necessity, for it helps us to a better understanding of one another. And it has proved effective, also, in treating both physical and mental illness.

Music is about life – and it is about living. In the forms in which we know it best, it is composed according to principles which are rooted in patterns of society.

This study brings music from its most distant beginnings to the present day, with the intention of keeping the reader always near music's origins. For the way people used to *feel* music is the point at which we all begin to feel it. The history of music is a record of how at different times people have felt about music.

The history of music is recorded in different ways: in musical works, in written evidence, and in pictures. In this book particular stress is laid on illustrations which have been chosen from many periods and from many sources. They show how artists in different fields expressed similar attitudes, and how techniques in one art are frequently reflected in another. Many of the illustrations are outstanding works in their own right. In search of material, the author visited art galleries and private collections in many parts of the world. He has tried to show how all forms of art are reflections of life in all its variety.

In this volume, the emphasis is not so much on individual musicians, as on music as a collective art. The great works which are part of our

3

general experience are shown as the result of communal processes. However, the musicians who represent the high peaks of creative achievement are given special attention.

Into the categories represented by chapter headings the reader should try to fit the music he performs or hears, in this way he will be able to build up a comprehensive idea of the progress of civilization. To be aware of this progress is also to be aware of a responsibility; that is, to be alert to the cultural needs of the world. More simply, that may be reduced to being alive to the needs of the world. The aim of the artist is to create, not to destroy.

1   Concert Hall of the Béla Bartók Academy of Music, Budapest; drawing by Gyula Gáll

Contents

Note: Technical terms shown in the text in bold type are explained in the glossary

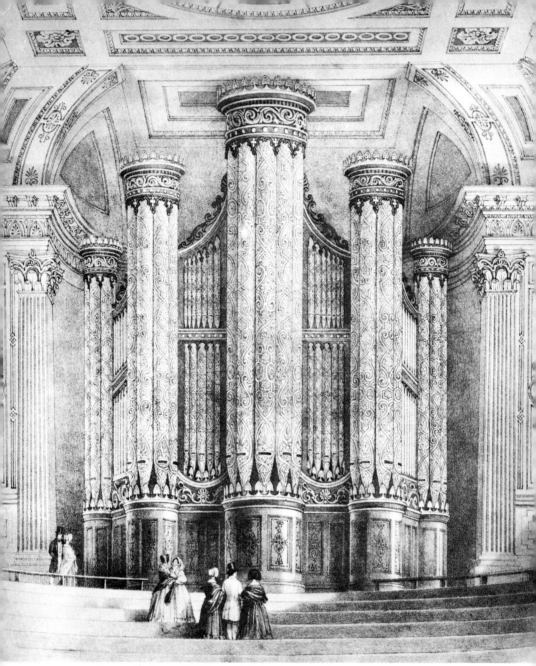

2 Organ built by William Hill for Birmingham Town
Hall, 1834; note the scale of the pipes and how they
form an architectural feature

1 How sound is made

THE HISTORY OF MUSIC is a record of the way in which man has made use of various sounds. When we say 'made use of' we understand that those sounds have been organized. And when we come to 'organized' we further understand that the world suggests purpose. When we say, then, that music is made up of sounds organized for particular purposes we are beginning to recognize what music is.

Sounds, an important part of our environmental experience, are a perpetual source of interest and fascination. To the extent that all of us are interested in studying, interpreting, and using sounds, we are all musicians.

For a long time, however, the art of music was narrowed down to particular kinds of sounds used in particular ways. From this process of narrowing down, what we now recognize as great musical masterpieces were created. But there came a point when many felt that the narrowing down had gone too far. There should be more freedom. The whole world of sound, and not only part of it, should be opened up for exploration. And that is where we are today.

What is called 'modern music' is sometimes condemned by those who were brought up on old principles and theories. It is frequently said that is is too loud, too dissonant, too unruly. The music of today, like everything else, is ever changing. It changes because there is a new awareness of the phenomenon of sound. Once upon a time the composer went out with a pencil and sheet of paper and tried as best he could to note down symbols to help him to recall those sounds that most interested him. Some composers still do this. Others, however, capture the material of music as it is, and preserve it on a magnetic tape.

The tape-recorder makes every man his own composer. For it is possible to arrange recorded sounds and to present the result as a piece of music. Why not? For what is music but 'organized sounds'?

But now we must find out what sound itself is. It is increasingly important for all of us to know something about the science of sound, which is called **acoustics**. In urban societies the atmosphere is polluted with undesirable sounds as it is by undesirable fumes. One experience is to hear a 'sonic boom' as a high-speed aeroplane passes overhead. A 'sonic boom' is caused in this case by the aeroplane 'crashing through the sound barrier', when the machine begins to go faster than sound.

This much we know because it is frequently spoken about. But it is only when we stop to think that we begin to learn that sound has certain properties. To begin with, it is somehow concerned with movement. At one speed an aeroplane does not make a sonic boom; at another speed it does. Sound travels at the speed of 1,100 feet per second, and when an aeroplane overtakes this speed (at 750 miles per hour) the effect of the sound waves piling up against each other is the 'sonic boom'.

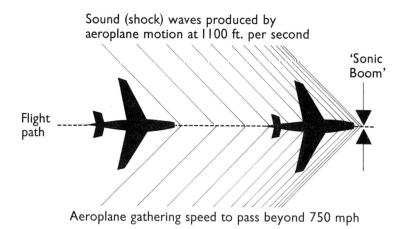

Sound (shock) waves produced by aeroplane motion at 1100 ft. per second

'Sonic Boom'

Flight path

Aeroplane gathering speed to pass beyond 750 mph

The opposite of sound is no-sound, that is – silence. And silence is sometimes linked with an absence of movement. In a famous passage in *The Merchant of Venice* Shakespeare speaks of the 'soft stillness' of the night. 'Soft stillness' was the setting for the sounds of music to 'creep in our ears'.

Sound begins when a vibrating force causes particles of air also to vibrate. Vibrations in the air take the form of waves and when these are received by the ear they give rise to the phenomenon described as 'sound'.

The strings of a violin may be seen to vibrate. These vibrations not only cause sounds, but particular kinds of sounds, to be heard. Such sounds are recognized as possessing certain qualities; of pitch, quality, and intensity.

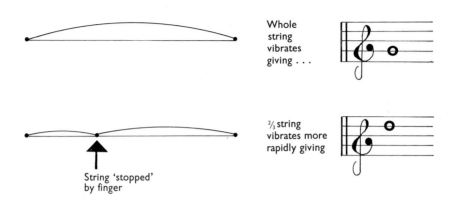

Whole string vibrates giving . . .

²⁄₃ string vibrates more rapidly giving

String 'stopped' by finger

Sounds are described as high and low. The difference between a high sound and a low sound is due to the fact that in the former the vibrations causing the sound are more rapid, or of a higher frequency, than those responsible for the latter. In the case of musical instruments (other than 'untuned **percussion**') the sounds we hear are created by vibrations of regular frequency. Where the vibrating agent causes irregular frequencies the resulting sound is described as 'unmusical', or, more rudely, as 'noise'.

Vibrations are reckoned for convenience according to the number of them occurring in a second. So the pitch which is represented by 'middle C' (on the piano) requires 256 vibrations per second. Higher notes need more, lower notes fewer vibrations.

The human ear is not able to receive more than a limited range of frequencies. The normal lower limit is about 20 vibrations per second, and the higher limit about 20,000. Even so it is quite difficult to recognize pitch accurately some time before these limits are reached.

Pitch is the first important property of sound so far as music is concerned, for it is on an accurate understanding of distinctions of pitch that melody is based.

A musical sound appears to us as loud or soft – or something in between. In order to produce a sound a certain output of energy is required, and the louder the desired sound the greater must be that

3   Flemish bell-founder of former times tuning a bell
to the vibrations of a violin

output. Scientifically, loudness is measured in terms of units called
decibels. These units of measurement have a wider application than
only to music at the present time. Modern man increasingly has to
learn to live with noise. Beyond certain limits of noise life becomes
intolerable, as is discovered by those whose houses are in the
neighbourhood of airfields.

We distinguish between different kinds of instruments, or voices,
because of their varying quality. In this connection it is often useful
to borrow a word with a meaning that originally had nothing to do
with music, but which can conveniently be applied to it. This word
is 'colour'. So we may, for example, refer to the 'colour' of the violin
and the 'colour' of the trumpet and agree that what we mean is the
particular quality of the sound produced by each instrument.

When vibrating systems which give rise to sound are set in motion
there is in every case one prevailing frequency. But within that frequency lesser frequencies occur. For instance, a string in motion will

vibrate as a whole, but within this movement segments of the string may also vibrate. The lesser vibrations stimulate sounds of higher pitch which, however, are incorporated within the one principal, or fundamental sound. The sounds of higher pitch are called 'overtones'. The occurrence of overtones depends on a number of factors, which include the manner in which vibrations are caused and the means by which they are amplified. The nature of different instruments will help further to explain this.

When sound travels it often runs into obstacles. If the waves meet a hard surface some of them at least bounce back towards their source. This is a familiar happening. A sound is created, and after a few seconds we may hear it for a second time. The primary sound waves have met with an obstacle – a wall, or a rock, or a hillside – and some of them have rebounded. The effect is described as an echo.

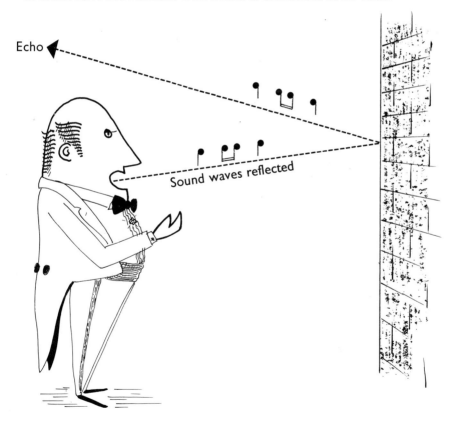

Echo

Sound waves reflected

Sound has other properties which form the basis for music. The principal ways in which sounds are organized give us melody, rhythm, and harmony. Melody is the result of putting together sounds of various pitch in such a form that they have a unified effect. In melody, one feels the balance achieved by clearly defined phrases, by the placing of the highest and lowest sounds within the phrases, and by regularity of stress pattern. This regularity of stress, together with the placing of accents, gives rhythm, which is, therefore, to be felt as a part of melody. A pianist may be seen to put down several fingers at the same time and sounds of different pitch are heard simultaneously. Effects arising from simultaneously produced musical sounds belong to the field of harmony.

But however science may analyse the behaviour of sound, the listener must interpret what he hears.

4   Drums of different sizes and various pitches, brass gong, ankle-bells, and double-reed wind instrument, played by the Wadigo people of Kenya

2 The infancy of musical instruments

THE OLDEST OF MUSICAL INSTRUMENTS is the human voice, but exactly how this was put to musical use for many thousands of years is not known. The earliest kind of music about which there is a considerable knowledge is that which has left behind material evidence of its existence. From all over the world instruments and representations of instruments have been recovered by archaeologists. These help to give some idea of the manner in which sound was controlled for musical and social purposes in very early times.

Today the general music-lover thinks of the music of Beethoven (who was born 200 years ago) as 'old'. How limited this view is, is shown by the fact that musical instruments used 10,000 years ago may still be seen in museums. This helps us to appreciate what an important part music has played in human society, and why it is that music as a social force still commands as much attention as it ever did.

As was suggested in the first chapter, the adventurous musician of today is interested in the exciting range of 'sonorities' (or musical sound effects) that are at his disposal. In this, as in other respects he is more in touch with the true origins of music than many of his more recent predecessors. Since it is now considered acceptable – even 'advanced' – again to make use of some of the principles of 'primitive' music, it is not unreasonable to assume that primitive music was not as crude as was sometimes thought.

History is taken to be the record of what is past, and it is sometimes thought that events rode on through time in an orderly procession. Civilization, however, does not work that way. Customs and usages which have died out in one community linger on in other communities. Cultural habits (in the broadest sense) are particularly liable to show an uneven pattern. So in the present context we find that musical instruments considered obsolete in one place are not considered obsolete in another.

We learn by experience that in connection with art 'obsolete' is a rather misleading word. For what has been described as obsolete can often provide a fresh experience of beauty.

5   Bukhayo horn, made from a buck's horn joined to a
cow's horn, from the Kenya-Uganda border country

Music begins with sound, and sound with vibration. The different
ways in which it was discovered that sounds were created and conveyed to the ear determined the main types of musical instruments.
These fell into four main groups which have been scientifically
defined by terms of Greek origin. The terms are as follows:

(1) **idiophone**
(2) **membranophone**
(3) **aerophone**
(4) **chordophone**

(1) Some materials generate sound more readily than others. Certain
types of wood, for instance, when struck with a hard object, give
sounds of a distinctive and musical character. So too do metal plates.
In each case the wood and the metal have particular qualities of
resonance, that is a capacity in themselves to amplify the vibrations
caused by an initial impact. In the case of a metal gong the quality
of resonance (of great importance to the growth of music) is easily
noticed in that the sound continues for a considerable time after it has
first been created.

Instruments of the idiophone group are many and varied. In the
percussion section of the modern orchestra there are **xylophones,**

6   Ivory hunting horn, 12th century, from southern
Italy

Chinese (or wood) blocks, castanets, cymbals, triangles, gongs, and
sometimes bells. Such instruments, which are often used for special
effects of colour, are directly descended from the earliest and simplest
of all instruments.

(2) When a stretched skin, or membrane, is set in vibration some
sound is to be heard. If however, the skin is stretched across a hollow
body the sound will be magnified. The body responsible is called a
resonator. The most familiar type of membranophone is the drum,
and the drum (of which there have been many kinds) also has a
venerable history. In the course of time many different kinds of drum
have been made, and even in the modern orchestra three types are
familiar – the kettle-drum, the bass drum, and the side-drum.

(3) In instruments of the aerophone family the two characteristic
features are a tube-like body containing a column of air and a means
of setting this column of air in vibration. The simplest way of setting
up vibration is to bore a hole in the side of the tube and to blow across
it. This is what is done with the orchestral flute. It is also possible to
set a vibrator in a suitably fashioned mouthpiece at the head of the
tube and by setting this in motion to stimulate vibration. The most
suitable agent was found to be a reed, or a thin and pliable strip of
wood (the 'reed' of the modern clarinet is in fact a strip of wood).
Sometimes two strips are bound together to form a 'double-reed',
such as is familiar in the oboe. In the case of a metal tube the lips
themselves may be pressed together to form a vibrator. This is what
happens with all the instruments of the so-called orchestral 'brass'
family – horns, trumpets, trombones, and tubas.

(4) When a taut cord or string is set in vibration some sound is heard,
but it is faint. If, however, the cord is fixed to a resonator (usually of

15

7 Welsh six-stringed crwth, made in 1742 in imitation
of a 14th-century instrument

wood) the sound is greatly amplified. The principle of the vibrating
cord fixed to a resonator (or sound-box) is that which characterizes a
vast number of instruments; those belonging to the violin group; a
variety of harps and lyres; lutes, zithers, and guitars; and the group
beginning with the ancient dulcimer and ending with the modern
piano. Observation will show that there are different ways of setting
strings in vibration; by using a bow (as is usual with the violin), by
plucking (as with the harp), or by striking with a beater or hammer
(which happens with the piano).

These four groups are the foundation on which experience of
instrumental music has been based since its known beginnings.

The materials out of which many instruments were (and are)
made are perishable. In the course of time wood, skins, and strings
disintegrate. So it is that the earliest examples revealed by archaeo-
logical research are only those which represent more durable materials.
The richest finds of ancient instruments which have a direct line
down to our own musical culture of today have been discovered in
the last fifty years in western Asia and the Middle East, in those lands
which are regarded as the cradle of civilization.

The great variety of these instruments indicates the richness of the
musical experience of the ancient world. The types of instruments
used were to be found in many former civilizations, and they continued to be used for thousands of years. Idiophones, membranophones, aerophones, chordophones, of one sort or another, are to be
found in the hands of musicians of Africa and Asia at the present time.
Sculptures and pictures show how in the past they were introduced
into the musical tradition of which we are the heirs.

3 Music and magic

LONG AGO those who had been leaders in their civilizations were buried with great pomp together with whatever it was believed they might need in a future life. Musical instruments were frequently entombed with their owners on the reasonable grounds that since music came from some other world, the ability to perform would be a useful accomplishment for those who were entering 'the other world'. The idea that music was 'sent from above' lasted for a long time, and even now is by no means quite out of favour. Science has provided sensible reasons for many things that once defied explanation, but nothing has as yet been put forward to account for musical genius. So musical genius – especially when it is shown by the very young – still tends to be ascribed to some kind of magical force.

According to the first book of the Bible, *Genesis*, the father of all who play the harp and the flute (formerly wrongly translated as 'organ') was Jubal. In Greek mythology the inventor of the cithara (a kind of lyre) and of music itself, was the sun god Apollo, or Phoebus. Music and the other arts and sciences were looked after by the Nine Muses, daughters of the god Zeus. Since Apollo was a son of Zeus (although by a different mother) the protection of music was very much a family concern. This was emphasized by the fact that Orpheus, son of the Muse Calliope, was also famous as a lute-player. This was, perhaps, not surprising since he was given a lute by Apollo. Many legends concerning Apollo, the Muses, and Orpheus, came down into later European culture. There are many statues and pictures of Apollo and his half-sisters, while the earliest operas concerned the legend of Orpheus.

The belief that music came from the sun was differently expressed in a myth long held by certain Mexican tribes. The god Tezcatlipoca, they said, commanded that a great bridge of whales and turtles should be constructed, across which music and musical instruments were to cross in safety to the earth.

But other peoples thought that music could also, perhaps, come from the moon. So a Turkish poet, Rawani, wrote of the harp in the sixteenth century that

> . . . in magic craft [it] is of great worth
> It brings the new moon down from heaven to earth.

Some musically talented gods were more versatile than others, and an Indian legend told how a great god named Lingo was not only able to play eighteen instruments, but could play them all at once. What was more, he was a master in each of the departments detailed on page 14; for he performed on cymbals, gongs, jingles, and rasps (idiophones); on the drums (membranophones); on horns and flutes (aerophones); and on zither and fiddle (chordophones). More of a specialist, the Japanese goddess of love, Benten, gave lessons to privileged pupils on the ôteki or flute. Nike, the Greek goddess of victory, was sometimes known as a lyre-player.

The Asaba people of Nigeria, who live on the west bank of the River Niger, until very recently held the belief that while music and dancing did not come direct from a god they were first given to mankind by a hunter who had learned them from the spirits who lived in the forests.

People often hold beliefs that sustain them. No one ever *proved* that music came from supernatural sources. At the same time it was clear that it exercised a powerful influence on human behaviour. It could lift man out of himself, enable him to forget his troubles and to join in companionship with others. Music helped man to work, to fight, and even to sleep. It appeared to give to him qualities which he otherwise would not have possessed. In the last few years scientists and psychologists working together have thrown much light on what happens to human personality under the influence of music. Certain kinds and combinations of sounds produce certain physical changes, as, for instance, in the raising and lowering of blood pressure. These changes in response to music show themselves in behaviour and also affect our appreciation of music.

In ancient times it was usual to ascribe what could not be explained in any other way to a 'god' or a 'spirit'. It was, therefore, reasonable to try to communicate with the gods or spirits by means of the very gift of expression which they had made available.

The gods who gave music also gave life and were especially to be praised or entreated at points of crisis in the cycle of nature. Some of

8   Benten, the Japanese goddess of love, giving a
lesson on the ôteki, or transverse flute; painting by
Kitagawa Utamaro, 1753–1806

the earliest lyres discovered on the site of the ancient western Asiatic
city of Ur are decorated with a bull's head. The bull was a symbol of
fertility and the music of the lyre was supposed to ensure that harvests
would be good. Other primitive instruments had different symbols
attached to them, or sometimes they were made in symbolic forms,
usually in the shape of animals. The great voice of the drum had a
special significance, for it was so awe-inspiring. The drum had a
place of its own in the ceremonies that societies invented to dignify
their appeals to the supernatural powers.

Ceremonies called for people who could organize them, and those
selected for such office were given special rank. They too were
frequently thought to possess extraordinary powers given to them by
supernatural forces, and their magical status was shown by dress and
decoration. Priests of many religious cults had their garments decorated with little bells, which added their own music to ceremony. The

priests of Assyria a thousand years before Christ and the High Priests of the Jews in Old Testament times wore bells. So too did Christian priests in Ireland until the Middle Ages.

It may easily be appreciated how music has an important role to play in primitive society. Even today workers in some African tribes are sent to their labours on the land to the sound of a flute. Since in the simplest forms of husbandry most forms of work have their own rhythmic pattern, workers will emphasize certain familiar rhythms through song, or even through the rhythmic sound of machete striking against machete. The ceremonies of harvest-time, and those connected with birth and death, with initiation into the tribe, of commemoration of ancestors, and wrestling-matches, are all surrounded with music.

Ritual music requires special instruments. Among the Ibos, as with other peoples, certain instruments are held to be 'sacred'. Those not of priestly rank are not permitted even to touch tortoise-shells (idiophonic instruments).

Ritual songs and dances are thought to enshrine the qualities of the gods who gave them and to whom they are given back. Sacred songs and dances, each with a special meaning, have powerful effects. When a whole community joins in and the music becomes louder and louder, and the rhythms more and more insistent, people may collapse into a state of trance.

The general pattern of ritual music – music for appeasing or pleasing supernatural powers – has remained constant from the earliest times. Tribal music still practised in parts of Asia and Africa, and among some descendants of Africans in Brazil and Haiti, helps us to understand to some extent what music was like thousands of years ago. Even in modern urban society the primitive impulse of ritual music is not quite lost. To some the organ is a 'sacred' instrument, only to be used in church. To others participation in a 'pop' music festival is a means of spiritual escape. Attendance at a symphony concert or an opera is not without its magic or a sense of ritual.

To some extent we are all musicians, in that we all can – and sometimes do – sing. But some sing or play better than others. Those who are specially talented win esteem from the society to which they belong.

Long ago rulers who wished to inspire the belief that they were invested with power from a god or gods, made it seem as much as possible that they were themselves godlike. They surrounded themselves with ritual which suggested the supernatural. They appointed high officers of State to supervise the ritual, and musicians, poets, and dancers, to invest it with a sense of mystery. Even today in England there is a musician with the title of 'Master of the Queen's Musick'.

Musicians, poets, and dancers were very highly regarded and some are known to us from ancient times because they were represented in sculpture, terracotta, wall-paintings, decorations on pottery, or mosaic.

9   Nike playing the lyre; detail on an Attic vase, *c.* 490 BC, found in Sicily

10   Girl dancing to the aulos, or double-flute, shown on an Italian vase of about 440–420 BC

The solo singer at the court of the Egyptian kings – as at every other court in early times – was a creative artist, responsible not only for singing but also composing the words and melodies of his or her songs. The singer praised the king, or the god, or both. He sang of the heroic deeds of the tribe. Singers were greatly favoured and enjoyed much fame. So it is that the names of some of the musicians of the early Sumerian dynasties have come down to us from nearly 5,000 years ago.

Instruments accompanied song and dance. They were also used independently. There is an Assyrian relief of the eighth century BC showing trumpeters blowing during the removal of a great statue. The trumpet-calls served a double purpose, to signal to the labourers when they were to haul on their ropes, but also to add dignity to the occasion and to salute the statue. Trumpets were blown in time of war, and on great royal occasions. Processions were accompanied with music from gentler wind instruments and harps. For dances percussion instruments came into their own.

The Bible tells us about music in ancient times in western Asia. The music of the Old Testament belonged to a tradition that was already a long one. It was music that was highly organized and full of meaning. Some part of this music has passed into the musical tradition which is ours.

11 The 'Dance of Death', a symbolic representation of the power of death shown in many forms from the Middle Ages onward; woodcut by Alfred Rethel, 1816–59

4 The beginnings of song

IT IS AN OPEN QUESTION as to whether instrumental or vocal music came first. But there is no doubt that it was through the regulation of the human voice that man first began to appreciate the finer differences between one sound and another. For it was by such regulation that he became able to communicate his thoughts with some degree of precision.

Sounds produced by the human voice have characteristics similar to those that we have noted in respect of instrumental sounds. Vocal sounds have pitch and they have quality. The most familiar sounds take the form of words, and when words are put into an order that can be understood, the continuity of speech is established. Speech is characterized by patterns of words which are emphasized or stressed in different ways. The stresses of language give rise to rhythm. So we may speak of the sound-quality of a language, and also of the rhythm-quality of a language. Taken together, sound-quality and rhythm-quality produce music.

Speech then is not only musical but it is music: music of a particular kind.

The rise and fall of pitch, which is called **intonation**, is an important element of speech. In everyday use of our own language we recognize how intonation adds meaning to what is said, often giving an emotional emphasis that would not otherwise be present.

In some languages, however, rise and fall is even more significant. In many African languages individual words have one meaning with one intonation, but another meaning with another intonation. This is the case, for example, with the Yoruba, Bantu, and Ibo languages. So marked is this that the intonations of words can be exactly transferred to instruments. So when drums reproduce these intonations – as they frequently do – they are described as 'talking drums'. Languages which are sensitive in this way are called 'melody languages'.

'Each language', said Zoltán Kodály, the famous Hungarian composer and scholar, 'has its own fundamental tone colour, its own *tempo* [speed], its own rhythm [system of stresses], its own melody: in

12   Singing children – choristers of St Thomas'
Church Leipzig at the time of J. S. Bach; drawing by
Ludwig Richter

short its own music.' The music of language has been the concern
of scholars and musicians for centuries. In the eighteenth century the
composer Christoph Willibald Gluck (1714–87), for instance, wrote
of the 'noble, moving, and natural melody of speech' and he tried to
make his own melodies come as near to this natural melody as was
possible. In the nineteenth century, Leoš Janáček (1854–1928), based
his melodic idiom on the stresses and intonations of the Czech
language.

There are many different ways of speaking. The more important
the subject the more deliberately it is spoken about. A speaker
describing an extraordinary event will try to invest it with a special
dignity. He will raise his speech towards song by means of a kind of
incantation. Even today the preacher often does this when reading
sacred literature aloud, and in many Asiatic and African countries the
rituals of society are conducted in speech-melody.

This is the point at which song began thousands of years ago.
Speech-melody gave dignity to social occasions. The exploits of heroes

Бавно-широко ((Largo)

Бе- ла съм, бе- ла,

ю- на- че, це- ла съм

све- та йо- гре- ла.

Бела съм, бела, юначе,
цела съм света йогрела.
Един бе Карлък останал
и той не щеше остана,
и той не щеше остана,
ам беше в могла утонал.
В моглона нищо немаше,
сал едно вакло овчарче.
Сиво си стадо пасеше,
с медно кавалче свиреше,
с медно кавалче свиреше,
с кавалан дума думаше:
„Галени га са ни зьомат
технону бално колко е!"

Je suis blanche, je suis blanche, ô mon brave ami! La
beauté d'une jeune fille a resplendi dans le monde entier. Seul un jeune berger,
enveloppé de brumes, n'a pas senti ce rayonnement. Il paît son troupeau et joue du
kaval: son chant conte la douleur des amoureux qui n'ont pas pu s'unir par le
mariage.

13   A folk-song from Bulgaria which tells of unhappy
love; note the shape of melody and pattern of rhythm

were recounted in suitable tones. In times of distress the emotions of a
community were given heightened expression by the proper vocal
colouring. The chief singer in a community, who was also poet and
orator, was a person of importance, as we have already learned.

In the *First Book of Chronicles* (9:33) it is written that the singers
of the Israelites were considered so important that they were freed
from other tasks, 'for they were employed in that work day and night'.

We are able to learn something of the origins of song by listening
to recordings of the simplest and most unsophisticated societies still
existing. The song-speech patterns of the Vedda people of Ceylon
and the Tierra del Fuego tribes of Patagonia show the limitations of the
range of intonation of primitive song. For in such song-speech the
pitch variations take in no more than two or three different, but
neighbouring, sounds. This characteristic may also be noticed in the
first attempts of very young children to sing. The way in which
children begin to use musical sounds does indeed tell us a great deal

about the beginnings of music. Here it may also be noted that the fundamental scale of European folk-music was one of only five sounds, for which reason it is called the **pentatonic** scale.

An important element in music, as has already been stated, is tone-colour, or **timbre**. A song is given additional significance by reason of its tone-quality. Here – since no two voices are alike in this respect – there is great variety. Types of timbre, however, may be cultivated. And they are cultivated for the sake of effect, to make the content of the song – the message, the appeal, the mystery – more important. All of this may be noted in the habits of present-day singers of whatever kind.

In the musical tradition of India the voice was reckoned to have three registers, each with its own characteristics. The sounds from the 'chest register' were said to resemble the roar of the tiger; those from the 'throat register' the cry of the goose; those of the 'head register' the call of the peacock. The first register was thought proper for the ritual song of morning, the second for those of noon and the third for those sung at sunset.

The more emotional song-speech becomes, the further away from everyday things it seems. The singer, therefore, tries often to cultivate qualities of sound that have an 'unworldly' character.

In the Near East a particular kind of 'nasal tone' is commonly practised. It is not uncommon for a singer to produce the wavering effect known as 'vibrato' by pressing on the larynx with alternate fingers. This practice is of great antiquity and was known to the ancient Assyrians. Other forms of varying the natural tone are practised. A familiar example is the yodelling of the Swiss and Austrian Alpine musicians. In some countries a nasal tone is, and was, intensified by the use of a **mirliton**, an instrument in which sound is created by means of a membrane in a pipe activated by the player's breath. At the present time the general use of the microphone in pop singing typifies the age-old desire to make vocal music a particular medium for affecting the emotions of people.

When a song is sung it is gone. Nothing remains. Our knowledge of pre-Christian music is at best sketchy and most of what is known relates to instrumental music, for instruments have survived enabling us to come to certain positive conclusions. So far as the songs of the earliest times are concerned, we are left very much in the dark.

14   Rory Vincent uses a microphone to intensify tone

The most important of early songs were those addressed to the gods. The Egyptians praised Isis the goddess of nature, associated especially with the moon, and her husband Osiris, the great giver of civilization. Osiris, also a sun deity, was the equivalent of the Greek Apollo. Isis and Osiris are familiar names to opera-goers because of the hymn addressed to them in the second act of Mozart's *Magic Flute*.

The Israelites sang hymns to Jehovah, of which we are reminded by the choruses in the Biblical oratorios of Handel.

The Greeks introduced vocal music into drama and solo singing alternated with chorus responses. One of the most interesting commentaries on vocal music in early times was made by the traveller and historian Herodotus in the fifth century BC. 'The Egyptians', he wrote, 'have . . . a certain melody, that is sung in Phoenicia, Cyprus, and other places also, although it goes under different names. It is like a Greek song and I wonder where the Egyptians got it from. It seems to me that it has been about from the earliest times.'

27

15 Sarastro, Priest of Isis, is praised for his wisdom at the end of Act 1 of Mozart's *The Magic Flute*, during the first performance, Vienna, 30 September 1791

The Greeks worshipped Apollo and two hymns to the god engraved on stone at Delphi in the second century BC have survived. In all, there are eleven fragments of melodies remaining from what must have been a large repertoire of song. But just as the theories of the Greeks concerning music formed the basis of later musical science, so too the melodies of classical Greece undoubtedly passed into a newer tradition. As Herodotus discovered, songs may in one sense have died, but in another they are continually being reborn.

5 Origins of Christian music

THE GREATEST SINGLE INFLUENCE on Western musical culture has been that of organized Christianity. It was the Church which, being for many centuries the only body actively concerned with science and education in all their forms, selected and reformed pre-existing music. It set up institutions to perform and protect a liturgical repertoire, developed techniques both of performance and composition, and established standards of judgment and criticism, all of which are, to some extent, still effective. Although the relationship, as we shall see, was often an uneasy one, music owes a great deal to Christianity; and Christianity owes a great deal to music and musicians.

Special bodies of singers and instrumentalists were employed in the Jewish synagogue, as the Old Testament informs us in many places. The music of the Jews was itself a combination of elements and practices accumulated from many sources over a long period of time. The first Christians looked upon themselves as still belonging to the Jewish communion. They took part in the rites of the synagogue and when they reached the stage of independence from Jewish worship they retained many practices and customs with which they had become familiar. This process of take-over was to repeat itself many times in the course of history, ensuring a continuity of traditions that could be achieved in no other way.

In a well-known passage in the New Testament (*Colossians* 3:16) St Paul speaks of 'psalms and hymns and spiritual songs'. The manner in which Psalms were sung at the beginning of the Christian era was without doubt the same as that which had been perfected in the synagogue.

The Psalms (see **psaltery**) were sung to simple, formalized chants; because of their already long ritual tradition they became and for long remained the foundation of Western Church music. The literary form of a verse in a Psalm shows two balancing phrases. This two-part form which was absorbed into music became independently important; much music of later date, both vocal and instrumental,

29

16 King David – to whom was attributed the book of
Psalms – playing the psaltery (a kind of zither); a 15th-
century Franco-Flemish miniature

was built on a basis of two balancing but contrasting sections.

Hymns were more free than Psalms in respect both of words and
music. The words at first were embellishments of and variations on
those of Psalms, and in all probability the melodies of the first hymns
were considerably more wide ranging than the strict chants of the
Psalms.

We should remember that although Psalms and hymns in one form
or another are familiar to us, those that belonged to Apostolic times
would seem very unfamiliar if we could hear them as first sung. We
should be particularly surprised, no doubt, by the nature of some of
the 'spiritual songs' of St Paul, for 'spiritual songs' were still less
restricted than 'hymns'. In older cultures and in the less advanced
communities of today the overflowing of gladness on the one hand,
and of sadness on the other, is found in improvised outbursts of
sound somewhere between song and speech. Such outbursts are
often incoherent, coming from a state of trance or ecstasy, and only
to be understood when interpreted.

As Christian ritual developed its own forms – centred on the Gospel account of the Last Supper, and memorialized in the Eucharist, or Communion – improvised elements were strictly disciplined. As Christianity gained strength it gave clear evidence of its identity in a distinctive repertoire of basic music and by a recognizable style of performance.

The Church first developed in the countries of the Middle East and then spread to North Africa and across the Mediterranean. The first Christian chants included many of Semitic, that is of Palestinian and Syrian, origin. In the fourth century Christianity was acknowledged the official religion of the Roman Empire and the process of making its rituals more formal quickened. Institutions of the Church and patterns of worship were at this time developed in different administrative centres of the empire, which had its Western and its Eastern departments.

Milan was one such centre, for it was here, by the Edict of Milan in AD 313, that the Emperor Constantine gave liberty to the Christian Church. Rome was another administrative centre of the Church, and by the beginning of the fifth century special bodies of priests charged with the protection of the music of the Psalms and hymns of the Church were in existence. At the beginning of the sixth century the great cathedral of St Sophia in Byzantium was built. Its dedication in AD 537 was a magnificent occasion and music was an important part of the ceremony. The Byzantine tradition of music included many elements – Jewish, Greek, Syrian, and so on – and this tradition affected what was happening and what was to happen in other parts of the empire.

By the sixth century morning and evening services, and the central service of the Mass, were directed by priests who often lived in monastic communities. Chants for Psalms, for versicles, and for responses, were formalized, and they were sung in **antiphonal** manner; that is to say, with one group singing one phrase and a second group singing an answering phrase in response. The pattern of antiphonal singing was, indeed, indicated by the two-phrase structure of the words of the Psalms.

Antiphonal singing gave contrast to performance and in one way or another it has had a considerable influence on the development of musical design and expression. During the sixth century other

31

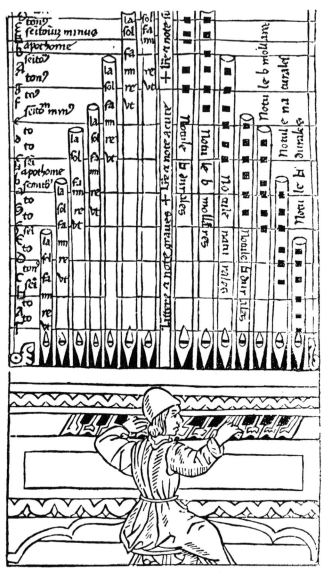

17   Medieval monk-musician, with useful information
on theory and sol-fa

developments were taking place and an enlarged repertoire of hymns from many sources – a large number, in Greek, from the Eastern part of the empire – was available.

Most of what is known about Early Christian musical practice is derived from accounts of Church ritual and from the texts of the hymns that have survived. One hymn, found in a third-century papyrus, in Egypt, was composed (or at any rate written down) by a Greek-speaking Christian. Below the words, a system of letters of the Greek alphabet, gave a clue to the actual shape of the melody. In the succeeding centuries various methods of preserving melodies were developed. These consisted either of letters of the alphabet or of signs intended to show melodic rise and fall. These letter signs (of which accents used in many languages today are a survival) were called **neumes**. In due course it was from these that the notation of modern music developed.

The first stages of the tradition of Christian music spread across a period of five centuries, in which it developed and was consolidated. This period was as long as that lying between the Reformation and today.

It is not, and will never be, possible to determine how many varieties of music were practised, rejected, or revived at that distant time, or their exact sources. It is sufficient to know that much attention was paid to music, and that principles regarding the place of music in worship and its structure were evolved. These principles and the music on which they were founded provided a firm basis for later development. So much was done, indeed, that it became necessary to review what had been accomplished and to bring together all the main strands of Church music. From the point of view of a great administrator there was a good deal of tidying-up to be done, for the Church now existed in many different countries with traditions of their own.

At the end of the sixth century a great reform of Church music took place. The author of this reform was Pope Gregory the Great, a fine organizer and administrator who was much concerned to end pagan customs that had been taken into Christian ritual in some places, as well as controversies between the Eastern and Western branches of the Church.

6 Musical missionaries

POPE GREGORY THE GREAT was the first ruler of the Church who systematically sent missions to different lands. He intended Rome to be the capital city of the Church in fact as well as in name; that what was decided there should apply everywhere. Since the fall of the secular Roman Empire in the fifth century (476), Europe had been in a condition of chaos. It was, it appeared, only the Church that could supply some sort of general order.

Missionaries went throughout Europe, and the most celebrated of them, Augustine, reached the shores of Britain. Augustine made friends with Ethelbert, the King of the south-eastern region of England, and became the first Archbishop of Canterbury. According to legend, Augustine and the monks who travelled with him, won the sympathy of the King and the interest of those around him by singing one of the Roman chants. The Anglo-Saxons then wished to hear more and to learn the new songs. However it may have been, it was not long before the natives were being taught this unfamiliar music, for the Pope followed up his first mission with a second. This time he sent sacred ornaments and manuscripts, so that the liturgy of the Church could be performed more properly.

Whenever a new style of music is introduced anywhere, it absorbs something of the style that, in part at least, it replaces. When Roman Church music came to Britain it had to find its own level among the traditions already established. These traditions, in fact, were the foundation on which the later achievements of Church music in Britain were based.

In Wales, long before Christian times, the Druids had organized musical events connected with their religious practices, and from these events the later tradition of the **Eisteddfod** developed. In Ireland musicians had been employed to chant poems, to the accompaniment of the harp, at the court of Cormac the High King of Ireland in the third century. In both Wales and Ireland the harp was to become, and to remain, a national emblem. The practice of singing heroic songs to harp accompaniment was carried on for many cen-

18   A Canterbury Psalter of the 8th century, showing
      King David supervising a team of musicians

turies at the courts of princes and chieftains in all parts of Britain, and
as late as the eighth century an Anglo-Saxon Bishop, St Aldhelm,
was making use of his skills as singer and harpist to persuade people
to come to hear him preach.

Because Ireland, being out of the way, was more or less unaffected
by the disorders that spread through Europe after the withdrawal of
Roman power, and because the country was Christianized in the fifth
century, a great cultural development took place there. Ireland

became known as the 'land of saints and scholars', and Irish missionaries went from their native land into England and many parts of Europe.

A Christian Church was organized in Wales before the third century and it remained independent of Rome for some 500 years. For a long time pagan customs and practices continued side by side with the new religion and the music of two or more traditions was somehow brought together. The Welsh people had always had a high reputation for singing. In the sixth century a Welsh historian, Gildas, told how the young people of Wales 'sweetly sang the praises of God'.

The joining together of Celtic and Anglo-Saxon poetic and musical strains at the end of the seventh century was symbolized by the story of the singer Caedmon, a monk at Whitby Abbey, as it was told by the Venerable Bede. Caedmon sang songs, which he himself had made up, about the adventures of the Children of Israel, the life and death of Christ, the Judgment to come, and many other subjects. He was, it was said, divinely inspired.

The missionary musicians from Rome were impressed by the singing they heard in England. It was their duty, however, to direct it to one uniform end. What happened to music outside the Church was, perhaps, no business of theirs, but inside the Church it was. By the middle of the eighth century, after many books and music-teachers had been sent from Rome, and local musicians had been trained in the way they should go, there was a high degree of uniformity in Church music. This was helped by the increasing practice of showing the pattern of melodies more or less exactly by means of musical notation.

Any consistent progress in learning or in the arts depends on social stability. And this in turn is the consequence of firm government. For several hundred years Europe had been in turmoil. In the eighth century this became less so. The strong rule of Charles the Great (Charlemagne) over an empire comprising parts of France and Germany encouraged a new concern for the arts of peace. About the year AD 800 there began a great renewal of interest and skill in architecture, sculpture, and the decorative arts and crafts, poetry, and music. Charlemagne realized that the Church could be a unifying influence, and that its organization made it the only one with men trained for the principal needs of society. He ordered the general acceptance of the monastic order founded by St Benedict – the

19　Musical instruments from a French Psalter of the
12th century

Benedictine Order – and from the end of the eighth century a great
many new monasteries were built.

Charlemagne's capital was Aachen, now in north-western Germany,
and here there are still to be seen some of the buildings which belonged
to the great complex of palace and government buildings in his day.
The style of architecture – a style which was general in Europe for
more than three centuries – was termed 'Romanesque'. This repeated
conventions of Roman architectural style, but also added Byzantine
and other Eastern features. The development of architecture was
similar to that of music. It absorbed influences and adapted itself to
circumstances.

Immediately before and during the Carolingian period there were
close contacts between the British Isles and Europe. Church music
was stimulated by the zeal of Irish monks who were to be found in

37

many parts of Europe, where they were responsible for founding many religious houses. Church music also benefited from the determination of monks who had been educated by the Irish. Among the most famous were Boniface called the 'Apostle of Germany', and Willibord, the Archbishop of Utrecht, who prepared the way for the establishment of singing-schools in northern Europe by their insistence on uniform use of the official music of the Church. This music was described as **plainsong** or **plainchant**. To make quite certain of its identity it is customarily called 'Gregorian', which acknowledges the work of the great Pope.

The headquarters of Church music was Rome. But to put into practice what was decided in Rome took time. In the eighth and ninth centuries there was a criss-cross of musical influences, all more or less coming towards, but sometimes drawing away from the central tradition.

Plainsong had become a central tradition because it was the only kind of music that had any kind of documentary permanence, the only kind that was supported by trained practitioners, and the only kind that had approval on government level. It was also important that in the new churches and chapels being built music was enhanced by acoustic features. Echoing and re-echoing in dark vaults and ambulatories (covered walking areas), the voices of monastic singers seemed to take on a new quality. It was easy to think that they came from 'another world', that they carried divine inspiration. The early administrators and philosophers of the Western Church paid special attention to music, which they both loved and feared.

Music came from God. But was there not also a music sent into the world by the Devil? The Churchmen of the Middle Ages were sure that there was. There were rude songs sung on unseemly occasions. Surely such music could not have been approved by God! What was worrisome was that the ordinary people seemed not only to like such music, but also to revel in it. This music was folk-music. For a long time it was badly spoken of by Church leaders. But, fortunately, it could not be killed off.

7 Song schools

FOR SOME 600 YEARS – from the time of Charlemagne to that of Martin Luther – the strongest single force in Europe was Catholicism. It was the Christian faith, as it was promoted by the organization of the Church, which not only gave such unity as there was but also provided reasonable arguments for such unity. Christian rulers more often than not differed among themselves, but they were agreed that it was the duty of all to defend their common civilization against the 'infidels' from the east. It was the Christian faith which encouraged the powerful to believe that they were divinely ordained to exercise power, and the powerless and poor to think that for what they had suffered in this world there would be more than ample compensation in the next.

The power of the Church was visibly expressed through great cathedrals and monasteries, built first in **Romanesque** and then in **Gothic** styles, which remain among the greatest of Western cultural achievements. Those who built these great churches were erecting monuments to a powerful social and political force, but they were also realizing the ideals of the saints, scholars, and mystics who were the architects of the Christian philosophy.

Cathedrals were awe-inspiring; they were also beautiful. In detail they were enriched with sculptures and on their walls were many painted pictures. Paintings and sculptures alike were inspired by a sense of the majesty of God, by a regard for the unseen force said to control human affairs, but they also spoke of a respect for humanity. Men and women were not portrayed as angels; rather were angels shown in human form. In later years, especially in the nineteenth century, the process (as far as this is possible) was reversed. This was to the impoverishment of art.

Churches and monasteries were islands of stability in times of turbulence. Those who lived in them were generally respected by those on the outside and for the most part they were able to go about their daily duties without molestation. The churches were for long the only centres of learning. They provided hospital and other social

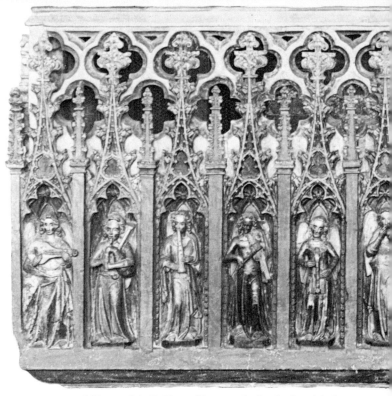

20 Minstrels' Gallery, Exeter Cathedral, with late
14th-century stone carvings, showing citole, bagpipes,
recorder, viol, harp, 'Jew's harp', trumpet, portatif,
gittern, shawm, timbrel, cymbals

services. They sponsored the arts. All this was done, however, within
a framework of ideology. The principles on which Christianity was
built in the Middle Ages were unyielding. Because of this and the
demands of those seeking greater freedom, the revolutions of thought
collectively known as the Reformation took place.

Christianity from the start was promoted to a large extent through
music. The great body of plainsong music that had been accumulated
over many centuries was a principal means of protecting the uniformity of belief. And it was very important that this uniformity should be
maintained. Plainsong, however, had developed in complexity. It is
true there were simple chants for the Psalms. But hymns had become
more free and more lyrical, while in settings of the single word
Allelujah musicians had allowed the ecstasy of melody to go further
than was possible when more formal texts were used. The ritual of the

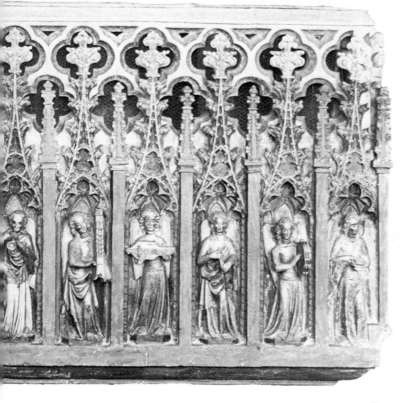

Mass and other parts of worship was as complicated as it was impressive. Music was an important – perhaps even the most important – part of it.

The only way in which such music could be properly cultivated was in foundations dedicated to its practice. The music of the liturgy was sung by specially trained priests whose whole education had been organized with the sole aim of fitting them to be servants of the Church. Church music was so important that the 'song school' was one of the earliest types of school in existence, and throughout the Middle Ages music was an essential part of the curriculum in any school.

For a long time the teaching of music was done by example. Boys listened to what their masters sang to them and repeated what they had heard as exactly as possible. Any errors, as the writers of those days tell us, were painfully corrected. Musical **notation**, as it existed, was imprecise and in any case manuscripts were so rare and precious that they could only be used by those in authority. At the beginning

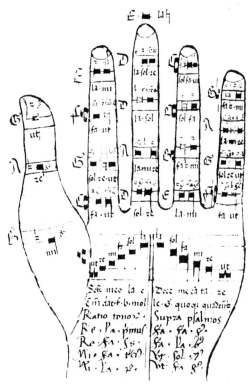

21　The Guidonian hand; a medieval scheme
supposedly derived from and illustrating the sol-fa
principles of Guido d'Arezzo

of the eleventh century, however, learning of vocal music was made much easier through the adoption of a system similar to the staff which we use today. The use of such a staff was promoted by an Italian monk and song-school master, Guido of Arezzo.

Guido was one of the most potent influences in musical education. He not only advocated the use of the staff but also of special syllables by which melodic intervals could be exactly appreciated and interpreted. These syllables (taken from the words of a Latin hymn) were used for many centuries and were revived in the nineteenth century in the **sol-fa** system. Guido also made use of hand-signs, to show differences in pitch. In this practice he also anticipated modern educators.

The development of a workable form of notation made many other advances possible. Among these the greatest influence on the future of music was the custom of singing in parts. Part-singing was certainly practised in primitive music, whether in Europe or anywhere else, and it is still to be heard in rudimentary form in tribal music.

But until musical sounds could be shown in visual form – on parchment, and later on paper – part-music could not be taken beyond a certain point. For this kind of music is complex and requires much thought for its development. Men learned to plan their musical ideas in writing. This is what has come to be known as the 'art of composition'.

The basis of early part-singing, then, was the performance of a melodic line in duplicate, with one voice parallel to another at a fixed distance or interval. By the time Gothic architecture was reaching its first climax as in the cathedrals of Beauvais and Rheims in France, Salisbury in England, and the choir of Cologne in Germany, the music of the Church, although still based on the traditional plainsong melodies, was already well advanced along the road to the kind of music with which we are familiar.

The melodies of plainsong were the foundation of Church music, but round these melodies others of freer character were poised, giving what we now know as **harmony** and **counterpoint**, and providing a texture of many-coloured sound. There were patterns in the intertwining of the ribs and arches designed by the architects. There were patterns too in the interwoven melodies of the singers. In both cases creative artists were trying to teach men to reach out towards an absolute state of beauty, or of goodness.

The Church was the centre of intellectual and artistic life in the Middle Ages. Those who looked after its music felt they had a special responsibility. For, as had been believed by all kinds of religious men since the earliest times, they held that music was the most 'divine' of the arts. Their duty was to protect it against the threat of the more ribald music of the outside world. Folk-music, however, persisted. Indeed it was bound to do so for the wish to make music is indestructible. Besides, singing and dancing were the most important means of relaxation amid the general monotony of life. Inevitably, folk-music borrowed ideas from Church music, and vice versa.

Side by side, and in large part with the same kind of music as the Church, there grew up a new tradition of music at court. In France and England especially the royal chapel became an important musical foundation in the twelfth and thirteenth centuries.

Those who had learned the art of music under the auspices of the Church began to put it to other use. During the time of the Crusades of the twelfth century an independent type of song grew up influenced by the impact of Middle East culture. Poetry and music came together in a new companionship and furnished the basis of the art of the **troubadours** of Provence and the **trouvères** of northern France. In Germany a similar enthusiasm for lyrical creativity led to the achievements of the **Minnesingers**. The principal Minnesingers, who worked in aristocratic settings but were at the same time affected by folk-art, are to be reckoned as the first song-writers of the German tradition. A famous early fifteenth-century manuscript in the University of Heidelberg contains hundreds of poems by the most famous Minnesingers as well as a sequence of illustrations as entertaining as they are instructive.

Sometimes Church musicians took more interest than their superiors thought they should in secular music, and in some cases actually composed music that was entirely secular. A few examples of such music remain, of which the most famous is 'Sumer is i-cumen in'. This thirteenth-century piece, written down in the thirteenth century, in the Monastery of Reading, England, has two sets of words. One could be sung in church, the other – a descriptive poem about the countryside – could not.

But that music of this kind could be composed at all was a tribute to the teaching of the music school to which this composer belonged.

22 (*opposite*) The words and music of 'Sumer is i-cumen in' as set down by a monk at Reading Abbey

44

8 Music and drama

DURING THE MIDDLE AGES when more time and more resources became available the arts developed rapidly both in techniques and in power of expression. They became more and more important within the framework of daily life. It is only comparatively recently that the arts have been allowed some kind of independent existence; and even today the duty of the artist to society is frequently debated. In former times it was the prime duty of the creative artist to 'glorify God'. So it is that almost everything that has come down to us from medieval times in the way of painting, sculpture, poetry, music, and their allied crafts, shows how much the artist was conditioned by religious ideology.

Manuscripts were decorated with illustrations, the walls of churches adorned with paintings, and windows filled with stained glass, to describe events and persons from the well-known stories of the Bible, or the once equally familiar legends of the lives of saints. Religion, however, was so built into common life that the actual world in which people lived was intimately linked with the conditions of past time and with the theologian's visions of Heaven and Hell. The artist required to depict a saint looked at his fellow man for inspiration, and so medieval art is full of vitality. Saints and angels, sinners and devils, often have a distinctly human look; frequently they are shown performing familiar tasks. As we learned about ancient times through pictorial representation, so much of the knowledge we have of early medieval music is derived from pictures and sculptures.

From the ninth century until the sixteenth century there is a wealth of evidence to show how extensively music was used to support the maintenance and spread of religious belief. The musicians surrounding King David in the Canterbury Psalter and those shown in the fifteenth-century windows of the Priory Church in Malvern, or the sixteenth-century windows in St Mary's Church, Warwick, England, and the paintings of the Flemish painter Hans Memlinc (c. 1430–94) give us some idea of the way in which musical sonorities were introduced into the service of the Church.

Religious ritual itself derived from many sources, and non-Christian elements were constantly being added. The painter looked around him and in drawing inspiration from nature and from the people he knew introduced a more human feeling into his art. So too did the sculptor and the wood-carver. But the oldest of the arts is drama, and one of the most important developments during the medieval period was the encouragement and development of dramatic performance as a further means of reinforcing the Christian faith.

Once the liturgy of the Church was formalized and placed within the setting of a great building, it became a form of drama in itself. Priests, symbolically robed, behaved like well-trained actors, playing their appointed roles and speaking or singing their given lines before the altar. The performance of the great central rites of Christianity was in itself a means of instruction and interpretation. It was also an art that was heightened in effect by the use of suitable music.

As far back as the tenth century some parts of the Christian story were stylized in a kind of poetic drama. The Holy Women going to the tomb of Christ on Easter Morning were represented by priests dressed as women; the Angel watching over the tomb was impersonated by another priest suitably attired. In a manuscript of the tenth century, the *Benedictional of St Ethelwold* (the property of the Duke of Devonshire, Chatsworth, England) the three Maries are shown being greeted at the empty tomb by the Angel. The artist was depicting this scene from life, from the kind of drama which the teacher-saint, Ethelwold, enjoined on the monks at Winchester.

'Whom do you seek?', chants the Angel. The Holy Women reply that they seek Christ. The Angel tells them that Christ is risen, and instructs them to spread the good news. Then everybody joins in a hymn of thanksgiving. This was the pattern of the Easter play which quickly became popular all over Europe.

The story was embellished and other characters added. Sometimes these extra characters gave the opportunity for comic relief. A favourite figure of fun was the gardener who supposedly looked after the ground where Christ's tomb was placed. To medieval people a gardener was a gardener and there was no reason why the gardener of the Resurrection story should be different from any other.

This pattern of illustrating the story of the Resurrection was adopted also for those of the Passion and the Nativity. By the

23 A musical scene in three parts; a triptych by Hans
Memlinc, c. 1430–94: I Angels with trumpets,
portatif, harp, viol; II Christ in Majesty, with singing

thirteenth century there were many sacred dramas, of more or less
elaborate design, which had taken their place as independent of the
regular liturgy. As the range of subjects increased, so too did the
ingenuity of authors and producers (but the inventors of these
dramas of course did not know these terms). There was a greater
concern for characterization, so that the figure of Herod, for example,
provided a model for the stage villain of later time.

The music for the first Church plays was sung in unison after the
manner of Gregorian plainchant. Greater dramatic effect was achieved,
however, when the practice of antiphonal singing – well established in
liturgical music – was introduced. Antiphonal singing, coming from
opposite directions, gives a kind of stereophonic effect and in the
lively acoustical setting of a great church is particularly impressive.
But dramas often required the participation of large groups – sometimes of men and sometimes of angels – and when this was the case
the singing was done by sufficient numbers to give proper dramatic
effect.

By the fifteenth century when the practice of singing in parts was
common, certain points in the drama were highlighted by choral
music of some complexity. Passion music with 'crowd' music assigned

48

angels; III Angels with psaltery, 'tromba marina'
(monochord), lute, trumpet, recorder

to chorus exists from the fifteenth century. At this time also Christmas
plays were made more popular by the inclusion of **carols**.

Carols were sometimes written in Latin, the universal language of
the Church that was understood by educated people all over Europe.
Often they were written in the mother tongue: in English, German,
French, or Italian. Sometimes they were in two languages, alternating. Both in words and music there was a strong influence from
folk-song and in many carols it is possible to feel the same striving
after naturalism that is evident in paintings and sculptures.

One of the most famous and popular of English medieval carols
was one of which there is also a beautiful modern setting, by Benjamin
Britten, in *A Ceremony of Carols*. This is the carol of the rose, of
which the first stanzas run as follows:

There is no rose of such virtue
As is the rose that bare Jesu
Allelujah!

For in this rose contained was
Heaven and earth in little space;
Res miranda

By that rose we may well see
That he is god in persons three
Pari forma.

49

During the later Middle Ages the boundary between Church and secular music became increasingly difficult to place, for musical skills were no longer developed solely by the Church. Kings and princes maintained their musical staffs, which included instrumentalists as well as singers. Many towns also had teams of musicians on the civic pay-roll. Trumpeters and drummers were necessary for ceremonial as well as military display. Players of wind and string instruments were indispensable for social occasions. They also performed in church when required.

In the more important cities the merchants played an increasingly important role. Banded together in guilds – which were trade associations – they went outside their purely commercial function and supervised many activities that formerly had been directly under the control of the Church. The guilds helped to control the organization of charity on the one hand and of entertainment on the other. Whatever they did, however, was done under the influence of the Church, since until the sixteenth century the religious basis of society was hardly challenged.

Religious plays were performed first in church, and then on a convenient site outside the church. By the fifteenth century the organization of the Church plays was handed over to the guilds. Until the Reformation, the plays occupied a great deal of the attention of the guilds, whose members not only found the preparation an interesting and often convivial business, but also a great means of promoting publicity for their own trades.

By the sixteenth century the Christmas, Easter, and Whitsuntide plays had departed from their simple origins. They were entertainments pure and simple, and were eagerly looked forward to. Giving opportunities to actors, and singers, and instrumental musicians, and painters, dressmakers, and carpenters, they provided the basis for a truly popular art. During the time of the Reformation in England and Germany religious drama earned the displeasure of puritan zealots. And so, gradually, it came to an end, to be replaced on the one hand by secular drama and on the other by the enlarged musical forms of the Renaissance.

24   (*opposite*) *The Nativity*, by Piero Della Francesca, c. 1416–92; detail of accompanied singers

9 Choirs and their composers

AT CERTAIN POINTS IN HISTORY the skills acquired by men and a great thirst for more knowledge and a greater understanding of the world have burst through the limits placed on spiritual enterprise by cautious authorities. One such point occurred in the thirteenth century, when the conservatism of the Church proved irksome to many. Among those who wished for change was Francis of Assisi. St Francis (as he was to become), who loved nature and was reputed to have preached to the birds, believed that Christianity was best taught by those who were as ready as he was to sacrifice wealth and personal comfort.

Having assembled a group of like-thinking men about him St Francis formed a society whose members were to go out into the world. In contrast to most Churchmen the Franciscan friars preached a joyful message and in so doing helped to bring a new note of gaiety into religious thinking.

There were other influences at work during the time of St Francis. In the thirteenth century other great men were born. They included the poet Dante, whose *Divine Comedy* is one of the great landmarks in European literature; Marco Polo, the great explorer who travelled into Asia; and Giotto, the first of the famous painters of Florence, whose works showed a new sense of beauty derived from a love of nature. In the thirteenth century the tradition of song composition begun by the troubadours in France and continued by the Minnesingers in Germany was also established elsewhere in Europe.

The spread of interest in secular song, for which an increasingly better educated aristocracy was primarily responsible, affected Church music. In Italy, a new body of hymns to meet the needs of a new age grew up. These hymns, or **Laudi spirituali**, were influenced by the songs of the troubadours, just as these had been at some stage influenced by the songs of the Church. In this way the two kinds of music, sacred and secular, that had formerly been regarded by the strict teaching of the Church as incompatible, were drawing together. That is how Francis of Assisi, who said that his followers should sing to God as if they were His 'minstrels', wanted it. And a closer relationship between sacred and secular music was beneficial to both.

People in authority, of whatever kind, rarely welcome change, and least of all in the arts. As we have already learned, the arts were regarded as influences for evil or good almost from the beginning of time. While it has never been exactly determined why this is the case, people have frequently tended to have serious moral doubts about 'modern' art. This is happening now, and it also happened six centuries ago. In 1324 Pope John XXII issued a statement in which he deplored almost every aspect of the music of his day.

But it was not possible to put the clock back. Already there were composers who had powerful protection from those who were in a position to challenge Papal authority in matters on which they considered themselves equally well, if not better, informed. Guillaume de Machaut (*c.* 1300–77), priest and civil servant, poet and composer, was able to practise the art of composition freely since he was in the service of the King of France.

In the earlier Middle Ages the names of composers, as of other artists, were not usually known. So it is that much music of that period is said to be 'anonymous'. By the time of Machaut, however, this was a thing of the past, and his name became well known. He composed songs and Church music and among the latter was the first known complete setting of the text of the rite of the **Mass** by a single composer. Machaut's setting was laid out in four vocal parts.

Another important composer of that period was Francesco Landini (*c.* 1325–99), a blind organist and song-composer who was a friend of Dante. Landini's gifts were generously recognized and he was greatly respected by the city of Florence where he lived and worked. In those days nationalism was not understood or considered as it is today. The use of Latin and a common form of religious observance unified the peoples of Europe so that it was possible for a man, particularly a scholar, to work happily in any country. John Dunstable (1400–58), the third great composer of the age, spent almost all his life away from his native England, and practically all of his manuscripts that remain are to be found in continental collections.

Dunstable composed settings of the Mass, **motets**, and also some secular pieces for voices. In these works he introduced harmonies that were richer than had previously been known in European music. Dunstable and Machaut laid down the main principles on which the next generation of composers were happy to base their techniques of composition.

During the fifteenth and sixteenth centuries the art of choral music made spectacular progress. However, Church music still had its basis in the traditional Gregorian repertoire. Around the most familiar melodies great structures of sound were organized, with individual singers (or groups of singers) being assigned separate and free-flowing melodic lines held together by common rhythmic factors. These structures came to be disciplined by the method of imitation, which had one part entering after another with the same melodic figure, by the regulation of discord within an increasingly concordant pattern, and by the sense of direction given by the maintenance within a work of a particular **mode**.

The opportunities created by the labours of many musicians across many centuries were eagerly seized by those who were best placed to take advantage of them. By the fifteenth century, the most important churches and cathedrals, as well as the royal chapels, maintained specialist groups of singers – boys, who were also given their general education by the foundations to which they belonged,

25 *The Assumption of the Virgin*, by Matteo di
Giovanni (died 1495); compare the drummer with the
player on p. 12

and men, who held office among the clergy and were specialists in
music. Among the musicians were also those who played the organ,
which was beginning to assume an importance of its own. Small
organs, called **portatif** (as had long been the case), were used in
processions, as is shown in many pictures; large organs, often contained in beautifully carved wooden cases, were termed **positif**.

Then as now it was expensive to provide the best music, so it is
not surprising that most progress was made where adequate funds
were available. In the fourteenth century the people of Flanders,

having achieved freedom from French domination at the Battle of the Spurs (1302), built up a prosperous state in northern Europe. Wealth came through the development of an international trade in cloth and was reflected in many splendid town halls, cloth halls, and religious buildings that are still the pride of modern Belgium. Under Philip the Good (1419–67), of Burgundy, the arts prospered greatly. Hubert van Eyck (*c.* 1365–1426) and his brother Jan (*c.* 1385–1441) painted the first masterpieces in oil, and there grew up round them a group of painters, including Roger van der Weyden (*c.* 1400–64), Hugo van der Goes (*c.* 1435–82), and Hans Memlinc (*c.* 1430–94), whose works adorned both public and private buildings alike.

Side by side with the painters there was a school of composers, in which Guillaume Dufay (*c.* 1400–74) and Jacob Obrecht (*c.* 1450–1505) were of special importance.

These composers were able to work with a considerable degree of freedom. They were employed not only by the Church but also by secular patrons and they enjoyed a high standard of living. They composed Masses and other liturgical music but they also composed **chansons,** or part-songs. The freedom from financial worry of these fortunate artists is reflected in a greater freedom of behaviour within the texture of their music.

The Flemings extended the range of choral music by making use (for the first time, it seems) of the deepest register of men's voices. They also delighted in weaving intricate patterns of counterpoint. Instead of relying solely on the melodies of the Gregorian tradition, however, they sometimes built their Mass settings round folk-melodies, and nobody appears to have complained. The music of these composers was sung in other parts of Europe with enthusiasm.

Jacob Obrecht was remembered for a long time on account of a musical version of the Passion story that was attributed to him. Much esteemed in Germany, this setting had a powerful influence on the German tradition of **Passion** music.

The great Flemish painters and musicians were part of a movement of thought that had been gaining impetus for a long time and which reached its peak by the beginning of the sixteenth century. This movement was known as the **Renaissance**. It was distinguished chiefly by a realization that in his own right man had powers of creation and invention, and the ability to search out many of the hidden secrets

of the world of nature. Among the great figures in Renaissance thought and art were Michelangelo, Leonardo da Vinci, Raphael, and Erasmus of Rotterdam. Leonardo helped to make even greater the cultural fame of Florence. Michelangelo (1475–1564) and Raphael (1483–1520) are the best known because of their paintings in the Papal Sistine Chapel, in Rome.

During the sixteenth century St Peter's Basilica was in process of rebuilding. The Renaissance Popes lived like secular rulers and, believing that power was to be effectively expressed through the work of great artists, they were generous patrons of the arts. The splendid musical gifts of the Flemings had long been admired throughout Italy and some musicians had spent periods of their working life at one or other of the Italian courts. Josquin des Prés (c. 1445–1521) for a time was a member of the Pope's choir. Jacob Arcadelt (c. 1514–75) was singing-master of the papal choristers.

The music of the greater churches of Rome was led by Flemish musicians until there were Italians adequately trained to take their

26 Fra Angelico, 1387–1455, *Christ Glorified in the Court of Heaven*; the central panel shows a very large body of angel musicians. The painters of this period tried to express the right quality of music for a scene

places. Italian musicians were not at all pleased when it seemed that all the best jobs went to foreigners. In the course of time Italian musicians were to find themselves resented in other countries for the same reason!

It was not only in Rome that Flemish influence prevailed. The first great Singing-Master of St Mark's Cathedral, in Venice, was Adrian Willaert (*c.* 1480–1562), a musician of great imaginative power. Although he only had seventeen singers at his disposal at St Mark's, Willaert knew how to make the most effective use of them. In 1550 he composed a set of Psalms in such a manner that they could be sung by two groups placed in two different galleries. From that time it became common to write music in many parts, that could be sung from different parts in a church or cathedral.

10 Fresh adventures in sound

WHEN, FOR THE FIRST TIME, Adrian Willaert sent his singers into the two organ-galleries in St Mark's Cathedral, Venice, to rehearse his double-chorus he was bearing witness to the fact that a further change had taken place in the status of music. By the middle of the sixteenth century the aesthetic values (that is, the 'beauty') of music were a matter of concern; in earlier times it had been its scientific nature that commanded most attention (in this context 'science' included all aspects of knowledge as opposed to the narrowed modern sense in which only technical matters are involved).

Reasons for the change of emphasis are not difficult to find. On the one hand, the influence of the Church had weakened; on the other, men had arrived at a higher standard of living and were becoming accustomed to, and also demanding, more in the way of luxury. Willaert's double-chorus, which stimulated other composers to write big-scale works for voices and instruments, set a new standard in luxury of sounds.

These works were for church performance, but the Church leaders at that time in many Italian cities were as much disposed to reckon the value of music by the pleasure it gave to them as by the instruction it might offer to others. The ruler of the Church lived then like any other ruler, surrounding himself with just as much in the way of pleasure.

In the Middle Ages the Church had been powerful in all respects of life and thought. During the period of the Renaissance, however, power began to pass from the hands of the spiritual rulers to those of an educated lay aristocracy. The Renaissance aristocrat made his presence felt by building and decorating palaces in a rich style.

The palace, whether in city or country, was not only a place in which to live. It was a symbol of rank and importance. The position of the aristocrat in society was further reflected in the number and quality of his other possessions, and in the number, bearing, and ability of those who he employed. However, there was more to it than this. The Renaissance man of property, unlike his modern counterpart, was expected to be able to do more for the arts and sciences than merely to pay for them. It was his duty to be something of an intellectual, something of an athlete, and something of an artist. Otherwise he was not a 'complete gentleman'.

Many books were written to advise gentlemen on how to be gentlemen. Nearly always it was strongly recommended that the student of proper manners should gain proficiency in music. Many music instruction books, therefore, were written during the sixteenth century and one of the most famous was by the English composer Thomas Morley (*c.* 1557–1603). This was *A Plaine and Easie Introduction to Practicall Musicke*, which was published in London in 1597.

The increase of interest in secular music and the desire to take part in its performance that characterized the sixteenth century made for a great expansion of what we would now call the 'music industry'. This industry contained composers, performers, and teachers (though a practising musician in those days combined all three functions), instrument-makers, music-publishers, and a number of subsidiary trades. The growth of interest in music also affected the other arts. Poets (who were often also composers) saw new possibilities for exploiting their talents, and for developing new techniques. The relationship between music and drama became closer, particularly in the masquerades and ballets that were expensively mounted at the main European courts. Painters and other craftsmen found new opportunities in the decoration of musical instruments. The music-room became an important amenity in the large house.

Musicians have at all times had to adapt their art to the environment. In the Renaissance period there was one kind of music for open-air display, another for the wide resonances of the church auditorium, and another for domestic use. It was the enthusiasm for music of the last category – **chamber music** – that led to a great expansion in the manufacture of instruments.

The instruments that were popularized during the sixteenth century remained in common use for a considerable period. Those thought suitable for indoor use – **viols** and **recorders, lutes** and keyboard instruments – were both rationalized and beautified. Viols and recorders were made in different sizes so that from each family (or from a combination of both) groups could be formed capable of playing the same notes that a vocal group could sing. A group of

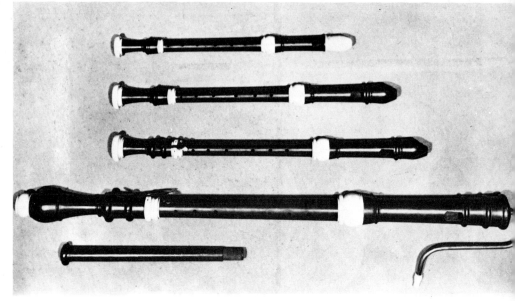

27 Set of recorders, made in the late 17th century to
play four-part music for treble, alto, tenor, and bass

players, of whatever kind, was termed a **consort**. Singers were often
glad of the help of an instrumental consort to help them sing the right
notes, or to stay in tune. Instrumentalists, on the other hand, often
played choral music independently and the earliest music for instrumental consorts showed many signs of its vocal origins.

The commonest instrument of the Renaissance period was the lute,
made in different forms and sizes. A young man of fashion was hardly
ever to be parted from his lute, which he used to accompany his
singing or to play independent pieces. The young man's sister, on the
other hand, when she wasn't listening to some other young man
playing the lute, was being taught to play on the **virginals**, or on the
larger **harpsichord**.

There were famous manufacturers of all these instruments in every
European country, although in almost every case the first impulse
came from Italy. Quite apart from their musical purpose many
instruments were so beautifully constructed that they became works
of art in their own right.

The debt owed by musicians to the Renaissance movement (of
which the prime inspiration came from a rediscovery of the thought of

28 Harpsichord, made by Giovanni Baffo of Venice in
1574, picturing Orpheus and the Muses

classical times) is often reflected in the decoration of instruments. For
instance, on the inside of the lids of harpsichords and virginals, scenes
from classical mythology were sometimes painted. Since he was a
musician, Orpheus was a favourite subject. In a short time the scenes
shown in this way were transferred to dramatic presentation, and
when this took place the new art of **opera** was born.

The development of musical instruments, which called for considerable scientific knowledge and technical ability, came about both
because there was an increasing demand for such instruments and
because of a general inclination towards scientific progress.

Music was revolutionized by advances on other technological
fronts; particularly in the field of music-printing. Towards the end
of the fifteenth century some religious music was printed in Germany
from wood-blocks. In the early sixteenth century the printing of
music from movable type was developed, while it was also discovered

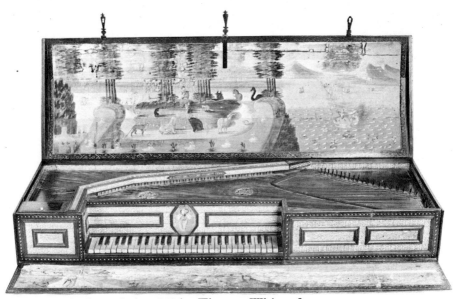

29 Virginals made in 1668 by Thomas White of
London, with a picture of Orpheus enchanting nature
in general

how music could most effectively be reproduced from engraved
metal plates.

The first famous music-publisher was Ottaviano dei Petrucci (1466–
1539), of Venice, who was granted a monopoly by the government of
the Venetian Republic at the beginning of the sixteenth century. The
next notable name was that of Pierre Attaingnant (*c.* 1490–1552), of
Paris, who published Church music, lute music, and volumes of part-
songs. By the middle of the century there were many publishers at
work in Germany, the Netherlands, and England, and through their
enterprise more music was available to more people than ever before.

Taking all things into consideration there was a great deal of
incentive for the musician. Flemish and French musicians continued
to exercise influence. Orlandus Lassus (1532–94), the greatest of the
Flemings, was for a short time Choir Director at the Church of St
John Lateran, in Rome, but his best work was done at Munich where
he was head of the music staff of the Duke of Bavaria. Lassus had
many offers to go elsewhere, but he remained loyal to his Bavarian
commitment. He composed Masses, motets, settings of Psalms, and
many part-songs. His music was found to be very expressive and its

popularity spread across Germany and into Britain to the north, and into Bohemia and Hungary to the east.

Like other great magnates of the time, the Duke of Bavaria devoted a considerable part of his budget to the arts. A great deal of money was spent on vocalists and instrumentalists for the chapel. But the 'chapel musicians' were not only employed for the purposes of sacred music. They provided music for pageants, for birthday celebrations, and for banquets, and many were able to supplement their earnings by giving lessons to the children of the court. Composers became more and more active on the secular front.

The greatest master of Catholic Church music in Italy was Giovanni Pierluigi de Palestrina (1525–94), most of whose career was spent in the Papal service in Rome. He composed much sacred music, but he also composed more than a hundred secular songs, or **madrigals**.

The madrigal grew out of an old popular form of part-song known as the **frottola**. In the Renaissance era composers were inspired by the poems of Francesco Petrarca (1304–74), Torquato Tasso (1544–95), and Lodovico Ariosto (1474–1533). Settings of the poems of these famous Renaissance masters by a large number of Italian composers from the time of Willaert to that of Claudio Monteverdi (1567–1643) provided models for many composers in other countries. A madrigal was usually written in contrapuntal form for four or five singers (varieties of madrigal-style songs, however, could have more or fewer parts), but it was so composed that the melodic patterns and the quality of the harmonies illustrated the words of the texts. Music now tended to be recognizable as 'sad' or 'cheerful', according to ideas existing in word form. So the madrigal composers – the most popular Italian composer being Luca Marenzio (1553–99) – helped to widen musical experience through new expressive qualities derived from poetry.

Madrigals were often accompanied by instruments. Sometimes madrigalian music was played by instruments alone. In this way ideas concerning emotional quality in music were transferred from one medium to another. One began to be able to recognize 'sad' or 'cheerful' music without the help of words.

Willaert is credited with the institution of double-chorus music. His demonstration that the acoustic and architectural properties of a

30 A Nürnberg trumpet-maker in his workshop;
engraving by Christoph Weigel, 1654–1728

particular building could provide the basis for a new consideration of
the art of composition stimulated a number of composers also
attracted to St Mark's, Venice. Of these the most famous were
Andrea Gabrieli (*c.* 1510–86) and his nephew Giovanni Gabrieli
(1557–1612). The Gabrielis wrote music for voices and instruments
often arranged antiphonally. The **sacred symphonies** of Giovanni,
rich and varied in their sonorities, were taken note of by the many
pupils who flocked to Venice from abroad. Among these pupils one
of the most important was Heinrich Schütz (1585–1672), the mag-
nificence of whose music was one of the glories of the Saxon court at
Dresden where he was **Capellmeister**.

The Gabrielis were also masters of keyboard music and composed
canzoni, **ricercari**, and **fantasias**, in which new modes of expression were essayed. Contrapuntal keyboard music, such as the canzona
and the ricercare, was almost indistinguishable from vocal music.
But in the free flow of ideas permitted in the fantasia the Renaissance
composers tried to provide for their patrons a more brilliant and
decorative form of music that at the same time seemed particularly

31 A choirmaster teaching the notes to his singers
from a single large music-book; engraving by
Christoph Weigel

appropriate to the medium. The Gabrielis and another Venetian
musician, Claudio Merulo (1533–1604), famous for his **toccatas** and
preludes, helped to fashion a distinctively keyboard style.

In the meantime the repertoire of keyboard music had been greatly
enriched by the music of Antonio de Cabezón (1510–66), the most
brilliant representative of the Spanish school of Court musicians.
Cabezón, who composed for keyboard, for harp, and for guitar, was
most esteemed for the marvellous way in which he decorated familiar
melodies, whether from folk-song or from courtly dance.

The period of the Renaissance, then, brought great changes into
the art of music. These changes came from a variety of reasons, all of
which, however, stemmed from a general desire to understand and to
make the best use of human resources then available. Music had been
thought of as a property of the gods. At this point in history – while
the qualities of music still seemed to suggest that something supernatural remained – it was taken over by man. As the next chapter
shows this was a process with many aspects.

11 Reformation

THE HISTORY OF CIVILIZATION is a sequence of struggles in which men and women fought in many ways to achieve greater freedom. These struggles concerned both material and spiritual freedom, and the two kinds of freedom often appeared to belong together. In 1517 a German monk, Martin Luther, began a campaign to reform the Catholic religion by nailing his condemnation of its abuses on the door of the Castle Church in Wittenberg. In this way the movement known as the Reformation began.

The Reformation focused not only on the need to liberate men's minds from false teaching, but also on the accompanying need to free them from paying money, which they could ill afford, for purposeless ends. To the peasants of Germany, Luther's campaign came as an inspiration, and they raised their voices not only against the greed and corruption of the officers of the Church, but also against the greed and injustice of their secular rulers. The battle hymn of the German Reformation was the **chorale**, or hymn, 'Ein' feste Burg' (*A sure defence*), which in the course of time was to become a national hymn. Both words and melody of 'Ein' feste Burg' were composed by Luther.

One aspect of the Reformation that was of great importance, was the claim of peoples to use their own languages for worship, in place of Latin which previously had been universal. Translations of the Bible that were made during the Reformation period in different countries were the foundation on which national literary traditions were to be built. The hymns that were written at the same time were also important in the tradition of literature, since they helped to stimulate a wider interest in poetry.

During the sixteenth century many collections of chorales were published in Germany. At first the chorales were prepared simply for congregational use, only the melodic line being printed. But before long chorales were arranged rather more ambitiously for four-part choir, as in the motet manner of composition. Chorales were not set in as complex a manner as many motets, but the same general prin-

66

32 The monument to Martin Luther in Wittenberg,
where the Reformation began

ciples prevailed. So the Reformation in Germany gave a great impetus
to choral singing.

As has been noted, Martin Luther himself was a keen practising
musician and so were his principal helpers. In those states which
adopted Lutheranism the general principles of Philip Melanchthon
(1497–1560) were put into practice. As it had been considered advis-
able for those who governed to be musically capable, so now it was
urged that those who were governed should acquire similar skills. An
expansion and intensification of musical education was a great factor
in the astonishing growth of German music during the seventeenth
and eighteenth centuries.

The Reformation was not the work of one or two men only. It was
a movement that had many roots. Lutheranism was one important
aspect of Protestantism. There was also Calvinism, a severe creed
with strict disciplines derived from the teachings of Jean Calvin
(1509–64) the French reformer. Whereas Luther loved music, Calvin
did not. For him – although he conceded that music was necessary to

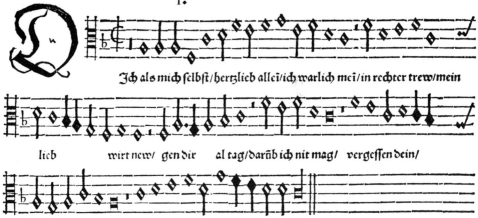

Ich als mich selbst/hertzlieb allei/ich warlich mei/in rechter trew/mein

lieb   wirt new/ gen dir   al tag/darüb ich nit mag/ vergeffen dein/

das hertze mein/fol vñ wil ftetz dein ey   gen fein.

33   Tenor part from a book of 'Good old German songs', issued by G. Forster in Nürnberg in 1539

rally loyalty to a cause – what was simplest was best. The characteristic music of Calvinism was settings of versified (or metricized) Psalms. The *Geneva Psalter*, of which the first edition was published in 1542, found favour among Protestants other than those who were Lutheran. The settings in this Psalter were the foundation of Anglican and Presbyterian hymnody.

Both chorale and metrical Psalm were intended to have wide appeal. Each drew from a broad musical background, and ideas from many sources were assembled. In the chorale and the metrical Psalm, melodies that were of sacred origin were brought together with those of secular origin. Secular in this context meant folk-song.

Folk-songs were a part of day-to-day living at a time when there was no great division between town and country. In the sixteenth and seventeenth centuries folk-songs began to play a part in regulating the nature of art music. Before this time the 'music of the people' had been treated rather disdainfully by Churchmen fearful of the possible moral consequences of some of the texts. Apart from the folk-songs that were changed into chorales, some were arranged for vocal ensemble in books of part-songs published in great numbers in Nürnberg and other south German towns, and still others were used as subjects for **variations** in the collections of keyboard music that were assembled.

68

The Reformation concerned human liberty. It was, however, not only personal but also national liberty that was at issue. The powerful forces of Catholicism were directed by the Habsburgs who ruled over Spain, the Netherlands, and many other European territories, and they had no intention of losing any of their possessions to Protestantism if it could be avoided. But the vigour of the Lutheran princes ensured that Protestantism would endure at least in the Lutheran States.

In the Netherlands – a colony of Spain at the time – an heroic people fought bravely and effectively against a cruel and typically ruthless colonial power. One of their leaders was the Count Egmont memorialized in a famous overture by Beethoven, who was himself of Flemish descent. In 1579 the freedom and independence of the Northern Provinces (now Holland) was guaranteed by the Treaty of Utrecht. Nine years later the cause of Protestantism was assured in England by the defeat of the Armada which had been sent by the King of Spain to subjugate the England of Elizabeth I.

The triumph of Protestantism, although its political consequences were different in different countries, gave a great impetus to the middle classes. Nowhere was this more marked than in England and in Holland, where merchants, manufacturers, and bankers, through enterprise and energy, brought a considerable prosperity to their own communities. The new rich acquired some of the habits of the aristocracy. They travelled widely and sought out culture in all its forms. And they became great patrons of the arts.

The vitality of the Elizabethan-Jacobean era in England is represented especially by the works of great dramatists, including Shakespeare, and musicians; that of the period of the Princes William and Maurice in Holland by masterpieces in the field of oil-painting. The works of Shakespeare and of the writers who were his contemporaries, and the richly descriptive paintings of many Dutch artists, gave evidence of the great part played by music in their respective countries.

Two great English composers worked across the transitional period of the Reformation: Thomas Tallis (1505–85) and his pupil and friend William Byrd (1543–1623). As in Germany, the changes brought about by the Reformation were helpful to music. Instead of composing Church music to Latin words, musicians were now able to

PARTHENIA

or

THE MAYDENHEAD

of the first musicke that

euer was printed for the VIRGINALLS.

COMPOSED

By three famous Masters: William Byrd, Dr. John Bull, & Orlando Gibbons.
Gentilmen of his Maties most Illustrious Chappell.

Dedicated to all the Maisters and Lovers of Musick.

Ingrauen

by William Hole.

for

DORETHIE EVANS.

Cum

Priuilegio.

Printed at LONDON by G: Lowe and are to be sould
at his howse in Loathberry.

34 The first engraved collection of English music for
virginals

use their own language in the texts of the new form of worship prepared for the Church of England. Tallis and Byrd wrote works to
Latin and some to English texts. The distinctive English musical
form of sacred music, developed from the motet, was the **anthem**.

Among the famous composers of anthems were Thomas Morley, Thomas Weelkes (1583–1625), and Orlando Gibbons (1583–1625), all of whom were Church musicians. At the same time, they worked sometimes for private patrons and sometimes, with interests in music-publishing, speculated on their own account.

Morley introduced the Italian madrigal into England and issued a collection known as *Musica Transalpina* in 1588. This was prepared because merchants in London had become enthusiastic madrigal-singers and Morley saw that the situation could be exploited commercially as well as artistically.

Morley was one of the liveliest of English madrigalists, of which there was a large group active for nearly half a century after the publication of *Musica Transalpina*. Weelkes and Gibbons were members of this group which also included John Wilbye (1574–1638), who often provided delightful studies of English landscape in the words and music of his madrigals.

English composers of the period were versatile. One of the most celebrated collections of music for the favourite keyboard instrument of the time, the virginals, is the *Fitzwilliam Virginal Book*. This manuscript collection, containing arrangements of anthems and of secular songs, of dances and folk-songs, variations and ricercari, toccatas and preludes, and even with some purely descriptive pieces, shows from how many sources music for private music-making was drawn. The Fitzwilliam collection, like many other manuscript collections both of keyboard and lute music, was made originally for one family. The first printed collection of keyboard music in England was that entitled *Parthenia* and published in 1613.

English composers were prominent in developing consort music, especially for groups of **viols,** and the tradition of the instrumental fantasia lasted until the time of Henry Purcell (1658–95), some of whose finest works are in this form. English composers were also active in the development of the solo song with lute accompaniment. One of the greatest song-writers of the period was John Dowland (1563–1626). The beauty and passion, and daring harmonic innovations of his work ensured for him a lasting reputation.

Dowland and many other British musicians were well received in Europe. Many of them, indeed, chose to follow their profession abroad rather than at home. Some for economic reasons; others, being

Catholic, because they feared persecution.

One of the famous English emigrants was John Bull (1563–1628), who spent the last fifteen years of his life in the Netherlands. An organist of the Chapel Royal, London, and one of the most renowned keyboard performers of his time, Bull was given the post of organist of Antwerp Cathedral in 1617.

The organs in Antwerp Cathedral were at that time in the care of the famous Ruckers family, who enjoyed an excellent reputation as manufacturers of musical instruments from about 1580 to 1670. Perhaps the first harpsichords ever made came from their workshop. It is Ruckers instruments that are to be seen in the majority of Dutch paintings which show musical subjects.

The great Dutch musician of the period was Jan Pieterszoon Sweelinck (1562–1621), organist in Amsterdam and friendly both with the Ruckers family and with John Bull. Sweelinck was a famous harpsichordist and organist. He composed sacred and secular vocal music and a good many instrumental works.

Middle-class interest was partly responsible for the characteristic development of music in Protestant countries. Sweelinck dedicated one volume of Psalms to the committee of an Amsterdam musical society, whose existence testifies to the wide interest taken in music in the city. It was also a time for popular and patriotic songs and many fine folk-songs (including the present National Anthem of Holland) were published at that time. The most famous collection was that compiled in 1624 by Adriann Valerius (1575–1625) of Middelburg.

Sweelinck wrote variations on some popular folk-songs and of these the melodies of a few were further treated in variation form by his German pupil, Samuel Scheidt (1585–1654).

The Reformation was effective in a number of northern European countries. It was significant not only from a religious but also from a political angle. During the second part of the sixteenth century the Church of Rome, having undergone several phases of reorganization, launched a counter-attack – known as the 'Counter-Reformation' – on the spiritual front. It was during this counter-attack that the Masses and other liturgical music of Palestrina were held up as an example of what truly religious music should be. The music of Palestrina, sung by unaccompanied voices, has a clarity of expression that is rightly reckoned to be incomparable.

After Palestrina's death, however, the Baroque style that distinguished every other part of cultural expression, increasingly influenced Catholic Church music, and very soon there was little distinction between sacred and secular music. In 1618 northern Europe was afflicted with a war that lasted thirty years. It was started by the Habsburg Emperor to reclaim lands lost to Catholicism. During these thirty years the most noteworthy advances in music were made in Italy.

35   Chamber music for voices and instruments in 1615;
painting on a spinet lid

12 Opera begins

M USIC DOES NOT EXIST by itself. It is always related to the society from which it emerges; sometimes indeed it is directly useful. Some music was associated with work, some with ritual, and at a later point music was created purely for entertainment. A creative musician – a composer – wants to express his own thoughts, but he also needs to provide what is required. In former times this problem did not worry the composer quite as much as today, because he was living among the people who needed his particular kind of music.

Composers are always looking for opportunities to increase their powers of expression. At certain times there seem to be more opportunities than at others – and it is then that new types or forms of music come into being.

One such time was the point at which the forces that had led to the Renaissance, then splintered into Reformation and Counter-Reformation, began to reassemble into a new pattern of artistic values.

Music had assumed a place in polite society without losing its roots in common life. As madrigalists and composers of songs with lute accompaniment were demonstrating, it had gained new powers of expression. Music enriched the words of the poets and in so doing stirred the emotions. The instrumental sonorities that were now being cultivated enhanced the various kinds of pageants and masques that were arranged by European rulers.

One generation takes things apart; the next generation puts some of the fragments together again, to form a new pattern. At the end of the sixteenth century, men were in a speculative frame of mind. It was the beginning of a new age. Before the Renaissance, ideas had been centred on the principle of God; after the Renaissance, it was the principle of ultimate human responsibility that counted. Music was moved out into the world.

Progress, of course, can only be measured by what has gone before. The great leap forward into the scientific revolution of the seventeenth century, represented by Francis Bacon (1561–1626), Johannes

74

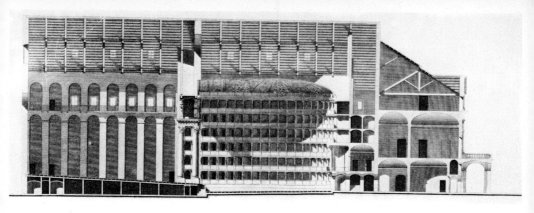

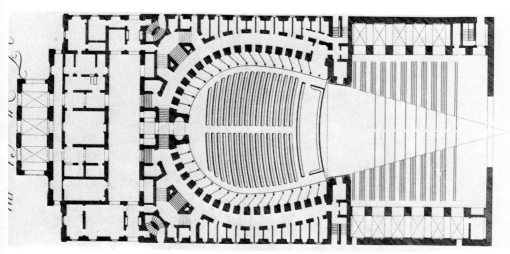

36 The most famous opera house in the world: La Scala, Milan, from a book to celebrate the building of 1778, which replaced a ducal theatre destroyed by fire in 1776

Kepler (1571–1630), and Galileo Galilei (1564–1642), was profoundly influenced by the wisdom of classical Greece and Rome. Rediscovery of the classical world made fashionable once again the legends and the myths of ancient times. The pre-Christian gods and goddesses became familiar through poetry and through painting.

It was the story of Orpheus, himself reputed to be both poet and singer, that especially attracted the attention of poets and musicians at the beginning of the seventeenth century.

In the sixteenth century the prevailing style in music was contrapuntal.

75

In the seventeenth century melody reasserted itself. People wanted to hear the beauty of one line of melody – a tune, that is – rather than the contrasting beauty of music in many parts. The melodic style allowed for greater flexibility and brilliance than could be achieved in contrapuntal music. In an age which was concerned with personality it allowed free play to the artistic personality of the solo performer, whether instrumentalist or vocalist. When these points are added together we reach the conclusion that the melodic style was better for expressing ideas of verbal origin and also personal emotions.

Simplification went back to speech-music, and the speech-music developed at the beginning of the seventeenth century was called **recitative**. Recitative was discovered as a useful means of giving vital information in the quickest possible time. But the capacity for emotional expression possessed by music had too little room to expand within the utilitarian recitative, even when this was accompanied by orchestra. In contrast to, but in association with, recitative, the extended melody form of **aria** was eventually arrived at. But to reach this point there needed to be a new relationship between composers and audience, and between them and the solo singers who were to play such a dominant role in the development of music during the **Baroque** era.

Experiments in bringing together words and music, action and music, and scenic representation, had taken place in different ways across many centuries. In Florence, in Mantua, in Venice, during the first half of the seventeenth century these experiments came to a conclusion in the acceptance of a dramatic-music combination that has (with many variations and against numerous attacks) lasted until our own time.

The earliest works in which drama was expressed throughout in partnership with words and music were based on the Orpheus legend. The part of the legend that was preferred related to the death of Orpheus' wife Eurydice, to Orpheus' desire to rescue her from Hades (the 'underworld' of ancient times), and to the fate of Orpheus after he disobeys the command of the spirits of Hades.

Of the first composers to make an opera based on this story the most important was Claudio Monteverdi. Monteverdi (1567–1643) composed Church music and original and expressive madrigals. But since he was a court musician at Mantua he was obliged to keep an eye on the kind of music-drama that was becoming fashionable for great occasions at Court. In 1607 he gave the first performance of his musical setting of the Orpheus story. The version of the story that he set to music had been prepared for him by another Mantuan court musician with a flair for literary authorship, Alessandro Striggio (c. 1535–c. 1595). Striggio provided Monteverdi with the **libretto** of the music-drama. From then on the partnership between musician and librettist was both important and delicate. Successful music-drama depends on a willingness to co-operate that does not always distinguish either musician or writer. Both parties also had to come to terms with the fact that in music-drama the arts of the painter and the designer were also of conspicuous importance.

La Favola d'Orfeo (The Story of Orpheus) was dedicated to and first privately played before the Grand Duke of Mantua. Soon afterwards it was performed at the Court theatre and in Cremona. All these performances were sponsored by aristocratic societies, called 'academies', of enthusiasts for the arts.

Monteverdi's *Orfeo* used some of the techniques of the madrigalists, and the instrumental sections recalled the character of the music of Giovanni Gabrieli. Monteverdi, however, made his music more clearly a means for conveying emotion. His melodic shapes and harmonies, and carefully suggested instrumental sonorities, appeared to give a greater intensity to the hopes and fears of the characters in the drama than was the case with other composers. The listener and spectator, in short, found himself absorbed in the drama, even personally involved. It was not: this is how Orpheus feels; it was: this is how I feel.

Monteverdi became Director of Music at St Mark's Cathedral in Venice, and in that city he found a great interest in music-drama. In 1637, the first of Europe's opera-houses was opened in Venice. This was known as the S. Cassian Theatre. Two years later the Theatre of St John and St Paul was opened. For this theatre Monteverdi, who had composed other dramatic works in the intervening years, composed what is now regarded as his greatest achievement – *L'Incoronazione di Poppea* (The Coronation of Poppea).

This opera, still part of the repertory, was the first that was centred on a historical and not a mythological subject. The story of how

Poppaea, with whom the Roman Emperor Nero was in love, came to take the place of the Empress Octavia, was taken from the Roman historian Tacitus.

Music-drama in its new form became popular in Italy during the first half of the seventeenth century at a time when most of northern Europe was at war. The rulers of the Church in Italy thanked God for their privileges and then proceeded to enjoy those privileges to the full. Members of noble families often became Cardinals in order to enjoy the dignities conferred on holders of that office. They did not, however, feel that it prevented them from enjoying the normal pleasures of aristocratic life, of which music-drama was one.

It was indeed possible that music-drama could once again play a part in the service of religious instruction just as it had done during the Middle Ages. During the Counter-Reformation the founder of the Oratory in Rome, St Philip Neri, had encouraged dramatic music performances based on sacred subjects. This special kind of music-drama came to be known as **oratorio**. During the formative years of opera, sacred music-dramas were popular in Rome.

In 1632, Giulio Rospigliosi, who later became Pope Clement IX, wrote a libretto based on the biography of a fifth-century saint named Alexis. The subject may have been from ancient times, but its treatment was up to date. The saint and the other characters in Rospigliosi's libretto were drawn from the familiar life of Rome as the librettist knew it. His opera, *Il S. Alessio,* was performed in the great Barberini Palace that had been built by Pope Urban VIII, from stones taken from the Colosseum. There were in those days many links with classical Rome.

A year after *Il S. Alessio* was produced, another music-drama was performed in the Barberini Palace. Based on a story taken from Tasso's colourful verse narratives of the Crusades – *Gerusalemme Liberata* (Jerusalem set free) – this was called *Erminia sul Giordano* (Erminia at the River Jordan). Once again the librettist was Rospigliosi. The music was composed by Michele Angelo Rossi, otherwise known as the composer of much keyboard music.

Erminia is more of a pageant than a drama. It has many characters and allows for impressive scenic effects (Apollo, for instance, is to be shown on a cloud accompanied by zephyrs, spirits of the winds). There is also scope for ballet. While the groups of hunters, shepherds,

37　Scene engraved in the original score of Rossi's
Erminia, 1637

soldiers, zephyrs, nymphs, and demons, clutter up the stage they allow
the composer opportunity to provide excellent choruses. In Rome
choral music was welcomed, as may also be seen from the libretto of
a music-drama based on the story of Theodora and published in Rome
in 1636. This music-drama had some influence, albeit indirect, on
English versions of the same story and eventually on Handel's
Theodora.

Italian musicians found many opportunities open to them and
when northern Europe had recovered from the worst effects of the
Thirty Years War, and when princes and dukes were anxious to
re-establish both prestige and privilege, there were few Courts where
Italian music-drama was not produced at least occasionally. Most
Courts also had Italian singers, instrumentalists, and directors on the
pay-roll.

One of the most important musicians of the day was an Italian, who,
having been taken to Paris as a boy, in time renounced his Italian
citizenship and became more French than the French. This was

38 A village band of oboe, violin, and hurdy-gurdy;
painting by Watteau's pupil Jean Baptiste Joseph
Pater, 1695–1736

Giovanni Battista Lulli, who came to be known as Jean-Baptiste
Lully (1633–87). Lully, who first danced in the Court ballets, became
in due course not only the Director of the Court Music for Louis XIV
but also an intimate friend of the King.

Lully's works were made in accordance with the taste of a brilliant
and sophisticated Court. Led by the King himself, the members of
this Court were accustomed to participate in pageants, ballets, and
even operas. Hence the importance of dance music and the pro-
liferation of airs, **minuets**, **bourrées**, **gavottes**, and **sarabandes** in
Lully's ballets. Lully was surrounded by a talented company of
French musicians and with their co-operation he established in Paris
a strong and independent tradition both of ballet and opera.

A friend of Pierre Corneille (1606–84), of Jean Racine (1639–99),
and Jean-Baptiste Molière (1622–73), Lully carefully studied the

relationship between the French language and French dramatic art and music, and in his operas aimed at a greater degree of dramatic effectiveness than was then to be found in Italian opera. Italian composers increasingly emphasized the importance of music in music-drama at the expense of the other elements. And within the music itself instrumental sonorities were undervalued after the death of Monteverdi.

Lully used string instruments with a new grace and charm. In a dance for Venus in the ballet *The Triumph of Love*, he even instructs the players to bow their instruments 'almost without touching the strings'. He also made a new kind of instrumental introduction to his operas. The 'French Overture', as this came to be called, became the starting-point for independent orchestral works. The 'French Overture' was enthusiastically taken up in northern Germany.

Musical development was in no small way influenced by political considerations and circumstances. So, because Charles II (son of a French mother) had spent years of exile in France, where he appreciated the Court music, French music was much heard in England after Charles's return to London in 1660. French operas were played at the Duke's Theatre in Dorset Gardens. Opera, however, enjoyed only an uneasy existence in England (where money was less readily available for it than elsewhere). The best dramatic music of Henry Purcell (1658–95), therefore, is contained in plays with music rather than in operas comparable to those of either the French or Italian composers of his day.

Among Purcell's more ambitious works are the scores of *The Fairy Queen* (1692), an elaborate series of masques loosely grouped round Shakespeare's *A Midsummer Night's Dream*, and of *King Arthur* (1691), a patriotic piece for which the text was written by John Dryden. Purcell's outstanding dramatic work, however, is *Dido and Aeneas*, a short opera for modest forces composed in, or about, 1689, for largely amateur performance. Beautiful though this work is, and immortalized through the 'death song' – 'When I am laid in earth' – of the heroine, Dido, to Europeans it seems no more than an off-shore footnote on the history of opera. This was an art that required massive subsidy. The English were reluctant to invest large sums in projects which seemed for the most part to be for the benefit of foreign artists.

13 G. F. Handel and J. S. Bach

GEORGE FRIDERIC HANDEL was born in the Saxon city of Halle, on the River Saale, on 23 February 1685. A month later, on 21 March Johann Sebastian Bach was born in Eisenach in Thuringia, some eighty miles or so westward from Halle. Handel, the son of a successful surgeon, belonged to a city that had a long musical tradition, and also a considerable intellectual reputation. Here, nine years after Handel's birth, one of the great European universities was founded.

Bach came from a family of musicians – town musicians, court musicians, and Church musicians – and was brought up with a pride in the family reputation. There was also a respect for the Protestant faith – if only because Eisenach had had its close connection with Martin Luther – and a sense of obedience to the local duke.

From his youth Handel was encouraged to take a broad view, and to look beyond the city boundaries. Bach, of more modest origin, was more closely bound to his environment. Both men made the best use of their opportunities and became outstanding masters of their art. Indeed they became the greatest musicians of the time in which they lived – the Baroque era. Handel left Germany to work first in Italy and then in England, where in fact he spent the greater part of his life. He became a European personality, whereas Bach, who spent the whole of his life in one German city or another, remained a local worthy.

In the course of time both came to be regarded as world masters because they brought together and expressed all the principal characteristics of the musical thought of their age.

Opportunity in many respects depends on accidents of geography. The Thuringians and the Saxons, rich and poor alike, had practised music of all kinds for centuries. They had a great love of choral music, and the Lutheran Church brought great benefits to music, especially as far as education was concerned.

The Lutheran ritual allowed for the performance of large-scale choral works, motets and **cantatas**, that were based on the universal chorale. The chorale was also the basis on which a large repertoire of organ music in the form of **chorale preludes** was founded. It was only in a state in which Lutheranism was the established religion that a composer was expected to write Church cantatas and settings of the Passion in which the chorale occupied a prominent place. Bach composed much music of this order, Handel practically none. In Italy Handel wrote some Latin Church music, in England he composed *Te Deum* settings and anthems, in both countries following the local tradition.

Because there were many opportunities in Germany to become musically proficient, there were many eager young professional musicians at the beginning of the eighteenth century. The majority of them were, to some extent at least, dependent on the provisions made for music by the many Court establishments. A musician learned 'German' music – that of the chorale and folk-song – in church and in social music-making. At Court he had opportunity to hear what was musically best in other national cultures.

German rulers were often ashamed of their German heritage. Anxious to appear cosmopolitan and abreast of the latest artistic fashions, they patronized French and Italian musicians. The young Handel heard music at the Court of Weissenfels, where his father was a surgeon. The young Bach knew what was happening at the Court of Eisenach so long as his father, a Court musician, was alive. Afterwards he was in one way or another in contact with the Courts at Lüneburg-Celle, Weimar, Gotha, Köthen, Dresden, and Berlin.

At the beginning of the eighteenth century influences from abroad were felt at these and other Courts. The overtures of Lully were widely known. The qualities of the French **chanson** were admired by intellectuals, and so too were the keyboard works of a number of distinguished French composers of whom the most important was François Couperin (1668–1733). So far as opera was concerned, the most famous name was that of Alessandro Scarlatti (1660–1725), whose stylized **aria** became the normal pattern for opera, cantata, and oratorio composers everywhere. Instrumental music in its most ambitious form was represented by the **concertos** of Giuseppe Torelli (*c.* 1658–1708), Arcangelo Corelli (1657–1713), and Antonio Vivaldi (*c.* 1675–1741). Torelli had once been Director of Music at the Court of Ansbach in Bavaria, and so his name was well known in that part of Germany. Corelli was a Roman composer who drew large numbers of eager foreign visitors to his performances because of his mastery of orchestral techniques. Vivaldi was a Venetian and also celebrated because of his orchestral mastery. They were among the makers of the modern orchestra, although they generally had at their disposal only relatively small forces of strings, harpsichord, oboes, and bassoons. On special occasions, however, they drew in larger resources.

In southern Germany Italian culture was greatly admired. In northern Germany the lucidity of French philosophy and art was a particular inspiration. These influences are reflected in many ways in the music of eighteenth-century Germany. Bach, for instance, entitled one work for harpsichord a 'Concerto in the Italian manner', and other sets of pieces for the same instrument 'French Suites'. Handel once composed a set of songs with French words in the style of a French cantata, and he composed some forty Italian operas!

The ambitious young musician in those days wanted to achieve success if he could as a composer of opera, for that was where the big money was. Handel was ambitious and so as soon as he could he left home. After studying law at the University and acting as organist at the Calvinist Cathedral in Halle, he went to Hamburg. There he played the violin in the opera orchestra and succeeded in having two of his operas performed.

From Hamburg, having raised funds sufficient for the expedition, he went to Italy. Here Handel managed to gain the favour of some of the most influential patrons of music and even some of the leading musicians. From Scarlatti and Corelli in particular he learned how to write both vocal and instrumental music that would satisfy the most critical audiences. The most critical audience of all, perhaps, was that of the opera-house. With *Agrippina*, a thoroughly Italian-style 'heroic' opera in the manner of Scarlatti which was played in Venice, Handel came triumphantly through a trial by public opinion. Throughout his life Handel owed the eminence he enjoyed to his wide public appeal, whereas Bach's reputation was first made among a more select group.

It was at about this time that a number of optimistic English aristocrats were hoping to establish Italian opera in the new theatre designed by John Vanbrugh in the Haymarket, London. When Handel brought his *Rinaldo* to the Haymarket, his success was as

39 St Thomas' Church, Leipzig, in the time of Bach;
here some of his greatest works were first performed

great as it had been in Venice.

London took to Handel, and he to London. Before long he was resident in the city and active in every department of its music. He composed music for state occasions, operas for the Haymarket Theatre, chamber and orchestral music, Church music, and works to display his talents as performer on harpsichord and organ. He joined forces with the music-publisher, John Walsh, and both composer and publisher prospered: particularly, Handel said, the publisher. Handel was also a conspicuous figure at Court.

Here again he was lucky. Since 1713, the English throne had been occupied by the Electors of Hanover, and there was a general disposition to favour those who were of German origin. The whole Hanoverian dynasty – from George I to Queen Victoria – considered that the only good music was German music and that the only good musicians were German.

This, strangely, was in marked contrast to the attitudes of their German relatives and fellow princes. In Germany, a German musician often had to take second place, a fact which caused much resentment.

85

40 *The Beggar's Opera*, a scene from this low-life
show painted by William Hogarth, 1697–1764

While Handel was becoming wealthy and famous, Bach was
struggling hard to secure a modest living for himself and his family.
After early appointments as organist, he joined the musical staff of
the Duke of Weimar. After nine years in Weimar he moved a little
way north to Köthen to become Music Director to the Duke of Anhalt-
Köthen. In 1723 he left Köthen on his appointment as Cantor of St
Thomas's School in Leipzig. The city administrators who made the
Leipzig appointment had not really wanted Bach. They had tried to
persuade two musicians much more in the public eye, Georg Philipp
Telemann (1681–1767) and Christoph Graupner (1683–1760), to
take the post. But each had refused. Telemann had no wish to leave
Hamburg, where he was Director of Music in the city. Graupner was
disinclined to leave Darmstadt where he was musician-in-chief to
the Court of Hesse-Darmstadt.

By the time Bach moved to Leipzig he had composed many of the
works which are now most familiar. These included many famous
organ pieces, particularly **fugues**, which Bach used to display his

outstanding gifts as a performer. In Germany he was widely acknowledged to be one of the finest organists of his day even if he was not similarly classed as a composer. Before he went to Leipzig Bach had also written the first half of the *Forty-eight Preludes and Fugues*. Designed to take the player through all the twenty-four **major** and **minor** keys made available by a new system of tuning, these works helped to widen the general appreciation of the tonal structure of music. Bach had also composed the **concerti grossi**, written as an offering for the Count of Brandenburg, which came to be known as the 'Brandenburg Concertos'.

The idea that an artist could have a private world of his own was not considered at all sensible in the eighteenth century. The wise musician became a realist. So it was that Handel recognized that to become a British citizen would be advantageous. In 1726 he became a British subject by naturalization and was immediately appointed a 'Composer to the Chapel Royal'. In this capacity he composed the anthems sung in Westminster Abbey at the Coronation of King George II, and other ceremonial music.

In the following year, 1728, a satirical play-with-music, which poked fun both at the politicians and the operatic fashions of the day, registered a great success in London. This was *The Beggar's Opera*. Handel was among those who enjoyed this entertainment, but he also saw that it threatened the future of the type of 'heroic' opera from which he made a large part of his living. Heroic opera was threatened in other ways. The aristocracy was fickle in its support. And the middle class disliked it more and more because it was in a foreign language, employing foreign and arrogant star singers. Finally, there was a reaction against moral laxity, to which opera was supposed to contribute in some way.

Handel gradually turned away from opera to oratorio and proceeded to make out of an already existing musical tradition a form that suited the British people.

Oratorio had branched off from music-drama and while it retained the main formal features of Italian opera it was performed in church in Italy and in the countries of the Habsburg empire. In Germany the church cantata was allied to oratorio in that it was based on the recitative-aria procedures proper to oratorio and opera. Passion music as it was composed during the seventeenth and eighteenth centuries was often distinctly operatic in manner. This was particularly true with the music of this genre by Telemann. The *St John Passion* and the *St Matthew Passion* of J. S. Bach, composed for Leipzig in 1723 and 1729 respectively, were dramatic rather than operatic.

Handel, however, saw that there could be a place for oratorio in a theatre setting in England. The ideal time was during Lent when ordinary stage productions were not allowed. There was another point. His friends wanted him to compose works to English libretti. So Handel decided this was his great opportunity. He conceived his oratorios theatrically, even though they had to be performed without action. But because he was not able to use all the resources of opera, he exploited one element that only played a minor role in opera: the chorus. It was the choruses of the oratorios that greatly appealed to the choral-minded British.

In the latter part of his career Handel composed some twenty oratorio-type works, including some which were entirely secular. Among these were *Saul* (performed 1739), *Messiah* (1742), *Samson* (1743), *Judas Maccabaeus* (1747), *Theodora* (1750), and *Jephtha* (1751). The most famous of these works was *Messiah*, which was first performed in the Irish capital of Dublin in order to raise money for certain charities. No work ever composed has so much won the affection of people the world over. In writing this work Handel was moved by a sense of compassion for his fellow-men and this at once was felt to be the message of the work.

While Handel was turning more and more to music with a sacred significance, Bach, in Leipzig, was more and more concerning himself with all the varieties of music needed in a German city. He composed Passions and church cantatas in the Lutheran liturgy, and motets for civic occasions. One of his greatest sacred works – the 'High Mass' (*Mass in B minor*) – was mainly composed so it could be presented to the new Elector of Saxony in 1723 in order to obtain a court appointment. Bach also wrote the secular music in honour of the new Saxon ruler. Much of his time, however, was occupied in attending to the affairs of the principal Leipzig music society, and he wrote a number of concertos for solo instrument(s) and orchestra for their meetings. These concertos occupy an important place in the development of orchestral music.

41 Small Baroque chamber organ in the
Church of Our Lady, Halle, where Handel
had his early lessons

42 Performance of a church cantata in Germany from
an engraving in J. G. Walthers' *Musical Lexicon* of
1732; Walther was a relative and pupil of J. S. Bach

Towards the end of his life Bach was recognized by many informed
musicians in Germany as a great master of the contrapuntal forms
that had come down and been developed over the centuries. In his
fugues Bach summed up what had gone before, but also opened up
new ways for the future. Two works written at the end of his life, in
response to manifest appreciation of his skills in the more difficult and
complex aspects of musical composition, were *The Musical Offering*
(1747) and *The Art of Fugue* (1748–50). These were composed after
Bach had visited the King of Prussia, at Potsdam, near Berlin, at that

43　A satirical drawing by Hogarth of a performance of
the oratorio *Judith* (1732) by William Defesch, 1687–1761

monarch's invitation. The King, Frederick the Great, was himself an
excellent musician who had composed a number of works. He enjoyed
Bach's visit and sent the old musician away full of ideas. Some of these
were incorporated in *The Musical Offering* and *The Art of Fugue.*

Bach died in 1750 and was buried in an unmarked grave, but he was
later entombed in St Thomas's Church. It was thought by most
people at that time that Bach was merely one Cantor among many.
Nine years later Handel was given what amounted to a State funeral
in London. A generation later both masters were given equal status,
the one complementing the other. They were the twin giants of the
Baroque era. They were more than that. They were among the
handful of musicians whose works affected the lives of people everywhere, irrespective of race or creed.

14 Haydn and Mozart in Vienna

To a visitor, Vienna is still one of the most interesting of the world's capitals. It is at one of the cross-roads of Europe, where east meets west and north meets south. It has fine buildings, many of which were designed by outstanding architects of the seventeenth and eighteenth centuries. Of all the great cities of the world it is the one with the best-known musical tradition. For some 150 years after the careers of Bach and Handel had ended, the musical life of every city in the Western world was affected by what happened to music in Vienna.

Vienna, seat of the Habsburg dynasty, was the capital of Austria and also of an ancient, loosely built, empire. The Emperor's rule stretched out southwards into Italy, eastwards through the Danube Basin into Hungary, Bohemia, and Poland. Although not all of its peoples were accorded equality, the Empire was indeed multi-national, and in eighteenth-century Vienna one would have heard many languages spoken and seen ample evidence of many traditions.

At the end of the seventeenth century the threat of invasion by the Turks, which had hung over Vienna for centuries, seemed finally to have disappeared. By the middle of the eighteenth century the Empress of Austria, Maria Theresa, having survived a long and costly war with Prussia, now felt that her realms were able to withstand any shock. She proceeded to give Vienna many of the amenities that were to make it one of the most attractive European cities.

Since the final relief from Turkish invasion in 1683, great architects under the leadership of Johann Bernhard Fischer von Erlach (1656–1723) and his son Joseph Emanuel Fischer von Erlach (1693–1742), had not only adorned Vienna but also the other cities of the empire with fine Baroque palaces, churches, and other buildings. Maria Theresa was anxious that her subjects should live in peace both with one another and with other nations. One of the means of ensuring peace at home was by developing a sense of pride that could unite people of many different national backgrounds.

In 1749, the Imperial Palace of Schönbrunn, near Vienna, was

44   The Prince's Palace in Eisenstadt, Austria, where
Josef Haydn spent much of his adult life

nearing completion. One day the Empress noticed one of the choir-
boys of the Imperial Choir – recognizable by the uniform worn by
members of the Choir – playing dangerously high up on the scaffold-
ing that stood against the Palace. To dissuade the boy from further
trespass, and to teach him that he was courting danger, the Empress
ordered the boy, whose name was Josef Haydn, to be beaten. The
master of the choristers, Georg Reutter (1708–72) was a good teacher
and a strong disciplinarian. Josef Haydn (1732–1809), and his brother
Michael (1737–1806), were among Reutter's best pupils; they also
had experienced his firm disciplinary methods, which, like his music,
were simple and effective.

Josef and Michael Haydn were of peasant origin and came from a
village in eastern Austria which was a meeting-point for various
ethnic groups. The Haydns spoke the Croatian language at home, and
in the countryside, but to their superiors they were required to speak
German. A poor boy with a good singing voice had a chance of
escaping from the poverty that was the general lot of the peasant in
those days. The Haydns became choristers in the Imperial Choir in
Vienna, and pupils at the cathedral school.

Not long after his escapade at Schönbrunn, Josef Haydn's soprano

92

45   The cottage in Rohrau, near Eisenstadt, where
Haydn was born; a 19th-century drawing

voice altered, and his place as head chorister was taken by his
brother. His mother would have been pleased if he had taken a 'safe
job', and become a priest, but Josef's ambitions did not lie in that
direction. He wanted to be a composer. So he earned a living in
Vienna as best he could, taking on all sorts of odd jobs. When he
thought there might be the possibility of performance he wrote
music.

Primarily, however, he devoted himself to studying music in all its
aspects. He looked carefully at the increasingly popular **symphony**
of which Georg Monn (1717–50) was an acknowledged master in
Vienna. He examined the scores of operas and of oratorios, composed
by his master Reutter and other Austrians, and Italians as well. Most
of all he was excited by the expressive character of the keyboard
sonatas of Carl Philipp Emanuel Bach (1714–88) that were beginning
to attract attention.

At the back of his mind, however, Haydn always had the sound of
the melodies of the countryside in which he had been brought up, and
the fascinating tone-colours of the music of the gipsy bands. Haydn
began to perceive that instrumental music could have a wide appeal,
and that it could by itself illustrate many facets of human life.

Haydn was a man of compassion and of humour, and his music seems to convey these qualities. He was a modest man and a religious man, and he was able to live a more serene life than many men of genius. Most of his life he was Director of Music to one of the richest and most influential families in the whole of the empire – that of the Esterházys. Although he worked in the various palaces owned by them Haydn was content to live for thirty years in the same little house in Eisenstadt, the town nearest to the village where he was born. Haydn had to spend much time in Vienna, in attendance on his patrons, and in his last years he had a house in the city, but he was really happiest in his own familiar and beautiful country.

The Princes of Esterházy spent a fortune on their castles. At the most important of their establishments – at Eisenstadt, and across the Hungarian border at Esterház – Masses and motets were performed in the chapel, and chamber and orchestral music in the now-fashionable sonata style, was played in the *salon*. Out of doors the wind band played when the occasion demanded. And operas and marionette plays with music were required for the theatre.

Of the operas composed by Haydn for the theatre which the Prince built at Esterház, the one which deserves mention is *The World on the Moon*. This was an **opera buffa** (comic opera) in which the story by Carlo Goldoni (1707–93), and the music by Haydn, make the moon appear rather more attractive than in fact it is. This work was written in 1777.

By this time Haydn's music was receiving attention far and wide. Publishers in Paris, Amsterdam, Leipzig, Berlin, and London, as well as Vienna, were finding it profitable to issue his works. His string quartets, piano sonatas, and symphonies, fulfilled the needs of many people for music, for entertainment, and self-expression through participation. They also represented acceptance of the emerging style based on the new type of **sonata** pattern. Sonata form now presented musicians with a set of architectural (or, rather, architectonic) principles that seemed indispensable for large-scale expansion. Sonata form was founded on contrasts of tonal centres and the logical development of melodic motifs that were themselves contrasting. The full sonata was a set of three or four movements of contrasted mood, the formal principles which gave rise to the generic name being most evident in the first movement but influential in the others.

While Josef Haydn was busily engaged on one side of Austria, his brother Michael was active on the other side. Dating from 1762, he had held the office of organist to the Archbishop of Salzburg. The ruler of a virtually independent city-state, like others of his class, the Archbishop maintained a large staff of musicians, some for the cathedral and some for his palace.

One of Michael Haydn's colleagues in Salzburg was Leopold Mozart (1719–87), a violinist and composer who had come to Salzburg from Augsburg, where Mozarts had previously distinguished themselves in other ways. One Mozart was a celebrated painter. Leopold Mozart's two children were already being spoken of as among the most remarkable infant prodigies when Michael Haydn arrived in Salzburg. Wolfgang Amadeus Mozart (1756–91), and his sister Marie Anna, or 'Nannerl' (1751–1829), were such gifted performers that they were soon ruthlessly exploited by their ambitious father.

In his boyhood, W. A. Mozart was taken to all the most important European Courts, so that his gifts could be profitably shown off. He met many important musicians of the day: Johann Christian Bach (1735–82) – J. S. Bach's youngest son and a writer of symphonies – in London; Giovanni Battista Martini (1706–84), a famous teacher, in Bologna; Christoph Willibald Gluck, the reformer of opera, in Vienna; and others. As he developed his skills, Mozart showed a dazzling mastery of every musical style of the period. He composed music with the greatest of ease.

Having gained an enviable reputation in boyhood, Mozart spent the rest of his short life discovering that it caused trouble. Because of jealousy he could not obtain posts which he felt he was well able to fill – in Munich, in Versailles, in Vienna – and had to put up with a minor appointment in Salzburg. That is, he put up with it until he could no longer bear the conditions imposed on him by a tactless and indifferent employer. At the age of twenty-five Mozart walked out of Salzburg and went to Vienna.

Here he had high hopes, for it was the magnet of the empire. From all over the Habsburg dominions princes came to the capital, where they had their town-houses. The nobility supported the numerous musical evenings that were so much a part of the musical life of the city and the opera. Their children were given music lessons in accordance with the cultural conventions of their class. Those who

46   The famous musical family Mozart

were skilled took part in chamber music and amateur orchestral performances.

Wolfgang Mozart was a famous pianist and he was a much talked about composer with a long list of dramatic works behind him. He had written works in the popular manner of **Singspiel**, and others that came in the class of *opera buffa* and **opera seria**.

When Mozart was in Vienna in 1782, he faced exciting prospects. He received encouragement from various sources. Joseph II and members of the nobility were pleased to commission performances of his works as well as new works. The German opera, *The Escape from the Harem*, was approved by Gluck (the greatest opera-composer of the older generation) and it became popular in theatres in the German States.

Gluck was a very famous musician in Vienna and throughout the Austrian Empire. His ideas were of great value to later generations of musicians, for it was on them that modern opera was built. Gluck believed that opera should be a balanced art form in which words, music, scenic effect, and so on, combine together without any one of them dominating. For the young Mozart, Gluck's approval was a great source of satisfaction and his ideas were very stimulating.

Even more encouraging, after the first intensive years of effort, was the welcome given to Mozart's symphonies and string quartets by Josef Haydn. In gratitude, the young composer dedicated to the older and much-respected musician a set of six string quartets.

Mozart, having left the relative security of his Salzburg appointment, was on his own. For an independent artist to make a living in those days was very difficult. Mozart was a prolific composer, and he had to be in order to support a growing family. Even so, his compositions did not bring in much money. Mozart's last years were very hard, and he died in poverty.

It is, astonishing, then, that among Mozart's greatest works of that period were two of the world's most famous comic operas – *The Marriage of Figaro* (1786) and *Così fan tutte* (1790). Written with wit and grace of expression, sparkling with melody and delicate instrumental colourings, these works are none the less critical in spirit. They are attacks, albeit lighthearted attacks, on the way of life of the often idle rich.

At this time, inspired somewhat by the music of Haydn, Mozart strengthened the expressive content of his instrumental music, and in his symphonies of 1788 – in E flat, G minor, and C major – appeared to open up a whole new imaginative world. The careless raptures of **Rococo** art and early **classical** music were over; a new age was about to dawn.

In the summer of 1789, a revolution the consequences of which were to change the pattern of the world's affairs, broke out in Paris. It was from this point that music began to acquire new characteristics derived from the prevailing spirit of the age. Mozart was not to live through the events that shook Vienna and Europe at the turn of the century. But the music that he composed seemed in many ways to anticipate the shape of things to come.

Mozart's last three symphonies were not composed for particular patrons or particular occasions, as symphonies then so often were. They were free-standing declarations of a musician's faith: to be heard as statements in their own right. In 1789, Mozart composed a quintet for clarinet and strings, and two years later a concerto for clarinet and orchestra. These beautiful works were written for a friend, Anton Stadler, who was a gifted clarinettist, and helped to establish the distinctive tone of this instrument among the acceptable instrumental sonorities.

In the last years of his life Mozart accepted an invitation from Emanuel Schikaneder, theatrical impresario, dramatist, and composer, to write the music for a fairy-tale opera that Schikaneder thought might prove a success with a Viennese public which wanted a change from the normal diet of Italian opera, German *Singspiel*, and pantomime.

The result, *The Magic Flute*, became one of the most famous of all operas. This work has characteristics of many different types of musical entertainment. It is, above all, a very German kind of opera, in which the music holds a great depth of meaning. Because it clearly defined new expressions in music it was soon seen to be the start of a new phase in opera, as well as a new phase in music.

After his death, Mozart was hailed as one of the greatest composers. Partly this was due to a change in the relationship of artist to society – the former now asserting his independence – and partly to changes in the manner of music presentation. These, however, were part of an even larger change – the attitude of man to man, and man to life. If liberty took on a new significance, in the New World as in the Old, Mozart and Haydn had an important part in the changing philosophies.

15 Increasing popularity of music

IT HAS ALREADY BEEN SHOWN how music was not only an art but also an industry. In the early stages of its commercial development it was concerned with supplying the needs of a more or less exclusive minority. For a long time, in most European states, opera and all forms of vocal and instrumental chamber music, were available only to a small and highly privileged section of the community. But, indirectly at least, they were subsidized by the underprivileged majority. The fine music of the Courts of France, Italy, Germany, and Central Europe, in the Baroque and classical periods, was in large part paid for out of general taxation. It was always the poor who could least easily find ways of avoiding the payment of taxes.

Princes and dukes rarely liked to be without music, as it helped to improve their reputations. When times were hard, therefore, instead of doing without music they merely omitted to pay their musicians. Nor were city authorities much different in this respect. Of this there are many examples. There are also pitiful examples of long-serving musicians on the edge of poverty writing debasing letters to their lordly employers asking for some consideration.

In 1651, Heinrich Schütz wrote the following to the Elector of Saxony:

> . . . I am not anxious to bother a Prince as illustrious as you with continual letters and memoranda. But I am obliged to do so on account of the hourly coming and going, continual complaining, and sorry condition of the wretched musicians in your establishment. They are indeed living in such distress that the very stones on the ground would weep. . . Most of them say that rather than bring dishonour to their most gracious master by begging they will go elsewhere. . .

Eighty years later J. S. Bach wrote to a friend that his employers, the Leipzig Councillors, were ungenerous and hard to please. If conditions did not improve he would have to look for work elsewhere.

In 1759, Josef Haydn thought he was well placed when he became Director of Music to a Bohemian nobleman. One of the terms of his

47 & 48   Master and servant: Nicholas II, Prince of
Esterház, and Josef Haydn, musician

contract, however, was that he should not marry. When he became
Director of Music to another nobleman, after the bankruptcy of the
first, he was thought to have attained the height of good fortune, for
he was now attached to the famous Esterházy family. Even so, his
terms of service were in some respects demeaning. He was, for instance, required to see that his table manners were sufficiently refined
to set a good example to musicians of lesser rank. He was expected to
compose music when asked to do so by his employer, but such music
should not be copied by anyone else. He should not undertake compositions for others except by permission of his employer.

For a man of less dignity and reputation than Haydn the terms
would have been quite degrading. Haydn made the terms meaningless
by reason of the fact that he came to stand higher in the world's
esteem than did his princely masters.

Haydn's fame spread rapidly and widely because the conditions under which music was promoted underwent a drastic change during his lifetime. The industry ventured more often into the public domain where, obedient to normal market forces, it operated according to laws of supply and demand.

The process of loosening the aristocratic control of music was a gradual one, but during the eighteenth century it gathered speed. This was partly due to the desire of a large number of people to enjoy a higher standard of cultural life, partly to the increasing desire for independence and some degree of security on the part of the musical profession, and partly to the opportunism of those who could see profitable prospects ahead. There was also the matter of improved communications. People could travel more easily, and so could information and ideas.

During the eighteenth century two kinds of musical society flourished; one was maintained by university students and teachers, the other by members of the business community. Sometimes the interests of these bodies merged, as was the case in Leipzig where the best-known musical society was directed by J. S. Bach. This position led him to compose many of his finest instrumental works, especially concertos for solo instruments and orchestra. G. P. Telemann, who had preceded Bach in the music-society activities of Leipzig, went on to Frankfurt and to Hamburg. In the cities he was very successful in putting civic music on a sound footing. He was an excellent businessman as well as a fine composer. His suites, concertos, cantatas, and chamber music, are a good index to the cultural standards of the cities in which Telemann worked.

Musical societies of one sort or another sprang up all over Europe, in both large and small towns. One organization that was to exercise much influence came into being in Paris in 1725. This was known as the 'Concert Spirituel' (Spiritual Concert). The title referred to the origin of the organization, which began by giving performances of what was thought to be appropriate music for the season of Lent.

The best performers from all over Europe were invited to appear at the Paris concerts. By 1754, the city was a centre of symphonic music, and the works of leading symphonic composers, like Johann Stamitz (1717–67), were not only played but also published there. In due course both Mozart and Haydn composed symphonies specially for French audiences.

In Britain the oratorios of Handel gave a great impetus to music-making. Outside of London the 'Three Choirs Festival' (so-called because the three cities of Worcester, Hereford, and Gloucester were involved) increasingly came to assume importance and influence. Also many other festivals were started. In 1784 a great Commemoration of Handel took place in Westminster Abbey. There were 500 performers and the effect of this, and subsequent performances on a similar scale, went a long way towards popularizing large-scale musical undertakings, and choral societies. A number of those who took part in the 1784 Handel Commemoration orchestra emigrated to North America and it was to musicians such as George Gillingham, violinist and concert-master, that America was indebted for its first orchestras.

After Handel's death, concerts of sacred music in public concert-rooms began to have a significant role in middle-class recreation. J. C. Bach and his friend and fellow *émigré*, Carl Friedrich Abel (1725–87), put symphony concerts in London on a sound basis, while similar concerts, supported by subscription, were given in provincial centres. Of these Manchester, Leeds, and Newcastle were the most important. Subscription concerts in the United States were developed, particularly in Philadelphia, New York, Boston, and Baltimore, and an important agent in their development was Alexander Reinagle (1756–1809). Born in England of German-Austrian stock, Reinagle learned to appreciate the methods of J. C. Bach in London. He was also acquainted with C. P. E. Bach. So when he emigrated to the United States in 1786 he was able to introduce many new ideas.

In Europe public musical activity was sometimes erratic. Rulers tended to find themselves involved in wars and under these circumstances were apt to reduce their involvement in music. However, when a war was over, so long as another did not seem imminent, there was usually a flood of good intentions to be seen moving towards the arts. In 1763, the Seven Years War, which had distracted a large part of Europe since 1756, came to an end. In that year J. C. Bach settled in England, while in Leipzig Johann Adam Hiller (1728–1804) took charge of, and reorganized, the concerts held in the great room of the Gewandhaus.

Instrumental concerts were given in theatres and in many other places of entertainment. Among these places those which drew the

49 *Dancing peasants*, painting by Januarius Zick, 1732–97
50 Music in elegant surroundings; painting by Franz Janneck

51 Learning music; according to a painting by Carle van Loo
52 Rehearsing an aria; a German musical year-book for 1782

greatest crowds were the 'pleasure gardens'. Sedate citizens took their wives to the pleasure gardens to eat and drink, and listen to the music, and their sons and daughters went separately to meet their girl and boy friends. The pleasure gardens also attracted less desirable characters. If music sometimes provided no more than a pleasant background, the fact that music was needed at all pleased musicians. It was in the pleasure gardens of London and Vienna that the works of Handel, Thomas Augustine Arne (1710–78), and J. C. Bach, Haydn, and Mozart were projected in a manner that would do credit to a modern public relations organization. What we now call 'great music' was not always listened to in silent reverence.

In eighteenth-century theatres and opera-houses, members of the audiences came and went as they pleased, bolstering their spirits during performances with food and drink. In pleasure gardens, audience attention was even more capricious. When symphonies of the classical composers were played, they were sometimes reduced to favourite movements, and even when such abbreviation did not take place,

104

there were frequent calls for movements to be encored.

The profession of music had always been a precarious one. Beginning with the eighteenth century, musicians tried to improve their conditions. In those days, when life expectancy was comparatively short and families were large, a major question for a household was what would happen if the breadwinner died. It was in order to meet this kind of situation that a Society of Musicians was founded in London in 1738. Handel helped in the formation of this society and both composed works and gave performances for it. In 1775 there was a similar society in existence in Vienna. Both these societies, which were followed by the rise of similar organizations in other cities, gave concerts to raise funds for the charities and thus they played a part in widening the opportunity for hearing music.

It was for the Vienna Society that Haydn composed his first oratorio, *The Return of Tobias*. In Haydn we meet the first composer who was really in a position to benefit from the changed circumstances within the music industry.

But for many years he was kept in his modest position by his princely employer, which did not really displease him. However, his works were soon taken up by various publishers. Among them the most important were Artaria of Vienna and Breitkopf and Härtel of Leipzig, firms which had been established to meet the growing demand for music and which, over the next century, were to publish some of the greatest music of all time.

Like other composers, Haydn obtained the best contracts from his publishers that he could. But when he was not able to travel he was greatly helped by the fact of publication. Haydn's music had been composed in a Court environment, but its appeal was general. The beauty and humour and originality of idiom and colour aroused enthusiasm in Berlin, in Paris, in London.

In 1790, Haydn was freed from most of his duties at the Court of the Esterházys by the death of Prince Nicholas. At the end of the year he travelled by way of Bonn to England. Here he was amazed at the amount of music given and also at the attention paid to concerts in the Press. Haydn spent a good deal of 1791 in England and he returned there for a further visit in 1794. It was for the London concert public that Haydn composed his last and most famous twelve symphonies. These works supplied a firm foundation for the repertory of the professional orchestras of London and the amateur orchestras of other cities.

The 'London Symphonies' contain some of the most popular of symphonic works, such as the 'Surprise' (no. 94), the 'Clock' (no. 101), and the 'Drum-roll' (no. 103). These titles, referring to descriptive elements within the music, indicate a broad outlook on the part of the composer. He was thinking of many people rather than a few.

In London Haydn heard some of the oratorios of Handel and this experience stimulated him to compose two oratorios *The Creation* and *The Seasons* which are among the few ever to be allowed to stand beside those of Handel in the choral society repertory.

Haydn was a countryman at heart. His devotion to his own native countryside is reflected in his frequent use of folk-song patterns in his works. But he grew accustomed to city life and to the ways of emperors and princes. In Europe he was a prince's musician. In England he was Josef Haydn, the friend of royalty but also of ordinary people.

The place of folk-song in the popular tradition and the growing interest of urban-dwellers in it was particularly recognized by an Edinburgh publisher, George Thomson (1757–1851), who commissioned not only Haydn, but also Beethoven, and Carl Maria von Weber (1786–1826), to make simple arrangements of British folk-songs.

53   The Subscription Rooms in Newcastle upon Tyne, England, built for Classical Concerts

16 The orchestra

THE TERMS **symphony** and **orchestra** are now so commonly used together that it is, perhaps, difficult to think of them apart. From what has gone before it will be clear that during the second half of the eighteenth century more and more works described as symphonies were being composed, and that orchestras were devoting more and more of their energies to playing them. Orchestral players were, of course, still employed in theatres and often in churches, but a new and important function was to provide music for concerts, both private and public. Programmes were usually of a miscellaneous character, but symphonies and concertos (in form closely allied to the symphony) were becoming their mainstay.

That is not surprising. A symphony was not one but several separate and contrasted pieces bound together by tonality, and also by the expectations aroused by certain familiar characteristics of style. The audience for a classical symphony knew that the first movement would be fast (preceded perhaps by a slow introduction), that the second would be more song-like, that the third would be a minuet, and the last would be a quick-moving, cheerful conclusion in the form of a **rondo**. A concerto contained three movements; the minuet, more or less obligatory in a symphony, was usually omitted.

In the classical period the symphony was thought of not only as a sequence of designs executed through sounds, but also as an expression of varying feelings or emotions. However much the composer might be interested in musical design for its own sake, he was never allowed to forget that his listeners expected him to say something that seemed to have a bearing on the way they felt. Music should be 'tender', or 'natural', and thoroughly expressive.

Music became more expressive through the use of additional resources and more advanced techniques. From the eighteenth century onwards, the virtuoso instrumentalist became increasingly prominent. So too did the idea that music should in some way become more 'lifelike'. This was nourished by music-drama in which realism, in various forms, was strongly cultivated. Thunderstorms without

54 Contemporary engraving of Handel directing
singers and instrumentalists in an oratorio

drums, hunting scenes without hunting-horns (*corni di caccia* as they
were called in Italian), or woodland glades without flutes providing an
illusion of singing birds, would have been unthinkable.

In the opera-house the range of musical effects was considerable. A
number of these effects were transferred to the concert-hall, with
sometimes startling results. In a 'hunting symphony' composed for
the entertainment of the hunting guests of the Archbishop of Salzburg,
for instance, Leopold Mozart (1719–87), the father of Wolfgang,
required shots from a rifle at certain points in his score. Some forty
years later Ludwig van Beethoven (1770–1827) wrote a symphony,
his Sixth, full of ideas 'drawn from nature'.

Seeing with one's ears, as it may be described, has always been one
of the joys of musical appreciation. It is an exercise that depends on
the association of particular sounds of music with particular events,
situations, or emotions. The great variety of instruments that produce

these sounds have at any time been too many for general use. When music became widely available through published copies, the structure of the instrument ensemble had to be simplified to a consistent layout of instruments, thus making many performances possible and greatly widening public participation in the musical experience.

In the seventeenth century the viol family – the foundation of instrumental ensemble – disappeared, and the violin family took its place. The more flexible and expressive group of violins, violas and cellos, supported by the double-bass, formed the basis of the Baroque period orchestra. This basic combination of strings was held together by the harpsichord. Recorders (gradually replaced by 'transverse' or 'German' flutes during the Baroque period), oboes, bassoons, trumpets, and drums were added when needed. During the time of Bach and Handel, apart from the foundation group of strings and harpsichord, there was no set scheme of instrumental layout for public performances. This may be appreciated from listening to the different combinations of tone-colours in the suites and concertos of the masters of the Baroque era.

Composers of this era were concerned with musical colours, as the works of Antonio Vivaldi and Telemann, as well as Bach and Handel show, but colour was not an end in itself. Baroque music was strongly contrapuntal, and in contrapuntal music the listener learns that the interplay of melodic strands within the texture is one major source of interest. The tone-colour of a particular strand is of less importance than the relationship of that strand with all the others in a piece.

In the nineteenth century some people misguidedly thought that Baroque music would benefit if more and richer instrumental colours were substituted for the originals. Arrangements of music of Baroque composers in an unsuitable idiom are still to be heard, but there is a general desire at the present day not only to restore the original colours and proportions to the lucid music of earlier times, but also to apply the same principles to contemporary music (see pages 152 and 156).

The classical reformation of instrumental ensemble, was, of course, a gradual process. It was as much based on omission as expression. In the preceding Baroque period the bassoons, for instance, had been kept going more or less continuously throughout a work, to give support to the bass line. In choral music the oboes too had been similarly overworked. In the symphonies of Mozart and Haydn the

55 Orchestra in the Opera House in Naples, in 1749,
from a contemporary picture

tone-colours of these, as of other instruments, began to be introduced
only when the character of the music made it necessary. This in fact
allowed the oboists and bassoonists more independence, while the
increasing popularity of the concerto for solo instrument and
orchestra encouraged a further development of skills on the part of the
player and of technical advances on the part of the instrument-
manufacturer.

Apart from his concertos for piano, Mozart also composed concertos for violin, organ, flute, oboe, horn, and clarinet. All these works
were important in that they helped considerably to establish the
credentials of those who played those instruments as well as the value
of the instruments themselves.

The clarinet, descended from the ancient pibcorn and for long only
distinguished by the coarseness of its tone, did not begin to show
itself in symphonic music until near the end of the eighteenth century.
Yet very quickly it began to assert itself as one of the most effective of
musical colours. The mechanism of the instrument was greatly

56 S. Koussevitzky conducting a performance of a
pianoforte concerto; painting by Robert Sterl,
1867–1932

improved and its tone turned into what we may now term 'warm' and
'expressive'. The clarinet is capable of a wide range of dynamics,
which made it suitable for suggesting 'romantic' ideas.

Mozart wrote works for the clarinet-player Anton Stadler, and
the composer's Clarinet Concerto and Quintet for clarinet and strings
occupy a place of importance in the history of instrumental music.

While Mozart and Haydn used the clarinet occasionally in symphonic music, Beethoven used it regularly.

Beethoven was regarded as a revolutionary figure in the history of
music. But perhaps the greatest revolution he wrought was in
indicating to those who attended his concerts that they should actually
listen to what was being performed. In the good old days of the
eighteenth century – as they must have appeared – it was by no means
uncommon for people of quality to talk all through musical performances. Beethoven made this impossible. There were those who
complained that his music was 'too loud'. If they had listened more
carefully they would have realized that so far as the orchestra was

concerned he employed a wider range both of sonorities and dynamics than had previously been the case.

During the first quarter of the nineteenth century, the orchestra expanded so that it could fulfil the needs of Romantic composers and also please the new middle-class audiences that heard the Philharmonic Society Concerts in London, the Augarten Concerts in Vienna, the Gewandhaus Concerts in Leipzig, the concerts of the Orchestra of the Concert Society in Paris. Principally, the great stimulus to orchestral playing was the works of Beethoven, which made very great demands on players. The aim of every conductor was to direct the Ninth Symphony. But, for a time, the aim of most orchestral players was to avoid playing in a work of such unprecedented difficulty.

By the middle of the nineteenth century, however, objections were less frequently heard, for by now techniques had so much improved that the difficulties of the music (great though they were) appeared less formidable. By this time the symphony orchestra was much larger. The basic string body (unsupported by keyboard) was one family; the woodwind another; the brass a third; and the percussion a fourth.

More than any other composer of the generation succeeding that of Beethoven, the French composer Hector Berlioz (1803–69), established the modern concept of orchestration. In 1830 he composed one of the most colourful of all symphonic works. This was the 'Fantastic' Symphony, a transference of autobiographic episodes from a dream into terms of music.

The orchestra, Berlioz said, should produce excitement and envisage the fantastic, like 'a hurricane in the tropics or the explosive roar of a volcano . . .' His book on the orchestra, *Treatise on Instrumentation*, published in 1844, was translated into English and German, and in 1904 an edition edited by Richard Strauss was issued. This was an influential book and in describing the constitution of his 'ideal' orchestra Berlioz specified more or less the instruments that would be needed for a large-scale work of the twentieth century.

The extent to which composers of the Romantic period were occupied in exploiting the colour potential of the enlarged orchestra of the period is shown especially in works like the 'Fantastic' Symphony which have descriptive titles. Such titles were fashionable. Among the more familiar 'programme' works which show the

André Previn directing the London Symphony
Orchestra

nineteenth-century orchestra to advantage, are Felix Mendelssohn's
(1809–47) 'Hebrides' Overture and 'Italian' Symphony, Robert
Schumann's (1810–56) 'Rhenish' Symphony, and the **symphonic
poems** of Franz Liszt (1811–86).

The development of the orchestra as a kind of gigantic instrument
on its own account led also to the emergence of the conductor as an
artist in his own right. In the eighteenth century the composer of a
work judiciously led its performance from the keyboard (*see* illustra-
tion 55), while the principal violinist also exercised a disciplinary
function. In Germany and in America the principal violinist, known
as the 'leader' in Britain, came to be called the 'concert-master'.

The pioneers of interpretative conducting were Sir George Smart
(1776–1867) in England, François Habeneck (1781–1849) in France,
and Louis Spohr (1784–1859) in Germany. Berlioz found his musical
philosophy in the works of Beethoven. Smart, Habeneck, and Spohr
regarded the proper interpretation of Beethoven as a first duty. The
next great figure in world music, Richard Wagner (1813–83), was
also profoundly moved by the revolution wrought in music by
Beethoven; and most of all, by Beethoven's revelation of his thoughts
and ideals through the medium of the orchestra.

17 The pianoforte

FOR A MATTER OF 200 years or so before the Classical period reached its zenith, music had developed in two channels. In the one was public music, often associated with particular occasions, and ambitious in scale. In the other was private music, played and sung for recreation. The two kinds of music, however, were interrelated, and the main trends evident in public music were soon to be seen in private music.

During the Classical period the impulses that were to distinguish the Romantic period began to assert themselves. Because of the urge towards a freer concept of society that dominated the thoughts of those who were dissatisfied with the way things were, there was a strong feeling for 'expression'. The orchestra, as we have seen, grew in influence because of its wealth of tone-colour and its potential for expression. By now it belonged to the sphere of public music. Private music during the Classical era was largely dominated by the keyboard instrument.

During the eighteenth century music was practised in most well-to-do households, and keyboard instruments were included in the furnishings. Sometimes a family owned a chamber organ, sometimes a harpsichord, sometimes a clavichord. Towards the end of the century, however, all of these were being displaced by the pianoforte.

The great advantage of the pianoforte in relation to other keyboard instruments lay in its range of expression. And this could be controlled by one player who – controlling so many nuances, or shades of expression – almost felt himself in possession of a private, one-man, orchestra. The pianoforte developed side by side with the orchestra and the changes in the one can be seen to have been reflected in the other. Beethoven's piano sonatas have a symphonic quality. His symphonies, on the other hand, may sometimes be felt to possess the virtues associated with the piano. Most of all, perhaps, in their percussive quality.

Beethoven's thirty-two piano sonatas, however, would not have been as they are had it not been for the craftsmen whose ingenuity

58   French engraving of an instrumental workshop of
about 1750

produced the kind of keyboard instrument for which they were
composed.

The pianoforte is a particular kind of chordophone instrument (*see*
Chapter 1) with strings – or, rather, wires – of differing lengths,
being activated by hammers. In the clavichord the strings had been
set in motion by metal tangents striking from below. In the case of the
harpsichord sound was produced through strings being plucked by
small quills or 'plectra' of leather. In 1709, an instrument-maker in
Florence, named Bartolomeo Cristofori (1655–1731), made a
harpsichord with hammers in place of plectra.

A German instrument-maker, Gottfried Silbermann (1683–1753)
who was much impressed by Cristofori's invention, built a number of
'harpsichords with hammers'. With an eye to their exploitation, he

showed them to Frederick the Great and gained his approval. The King had two of Silbermann's instruments installed at his palace at Potsdam. J. S. Bach knew Silbermann, who had built some of the best organs in Germany. Among those still to be heard are the instruments in the cathedral in Freiberg – Silbermann's native city – and in the Catholic Court church (now cathedral) in nearby Dresden.

One pupil of Silbermann, Johannes Zumpe, went to London, where he worked for a time with another immigrant instrument-maker, the Swiss Burkhardt Tschudi. Tschudi's partner and son-in-law, was John Broadwood. Zumpe and Broadwood went their separate ways and each contributed greatly to the popularization of the piano-forte both as a concert and a household instrument. Zumpe was particularly successful in making what might be described perhaps as 'family pianos', and the 'square pianos' he manufactured (sometimes in partnership with Gabriel Buntebart) provided a model for others to imitate. In those days piano models excited as much interest as models of cars today.

Meanwhile, a notable family of instrument-makers was establish-ing the pianoforte in Vienna. Johann Andreas Stein (1728–92), a native of Augsburg, was ingenious in designing new mechanical devices whether for organ or harpsichord. He was also a good musician. When, inspired by Silbermann, he turned to the manufacture of pianofortes, he paid particular attention to the qualities sought by composers. Stein's pianos were admired by Mozart and also by Beethoven. Of his inventions the most important was a pedal device for shifting the hammers away from the three strings arranged for each note in the piano so that they hit only one. This action was described as *una corda* and so it is that when the composer now wishes the player to use the so-called 'soft pedal' he indicates it by inscribing *una corda* into the music.

In the late years of the eighteenth century many attempts to increase the tone-colour resources of the piano were made. In some instances harpsichords and pianos were combined into hybrid instruments. In other cases percussion effects were operated by pedals. The 'soft pedal' was one device that survived. The other that came to exercise an influence over the character of music for the piano was that which is often incorrectly termed the 'loud pedal'. Properly this is a device for sustaining tone, by keeping the dampers raised that normally

59 Square pianoforte made in London in 1775 by
Johann Zumpe and Gabriel Buntebart

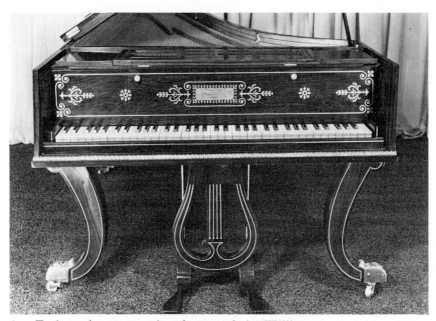

60 Early 19th-century pianoforte made by William
Stodart, whose firm patented the principle of the iron
frame in 1820

fall back on the strings after the release of keys by the pianist at the appointed end of note-durations. The introduction of a sustaining pedal was one more indication of the growing importance of harmony in musical expression.

During these years of experiment, pianos were manufactured in America, particularly in Philadelphia and Boston. In the 1820s, inventions by Alpheus Babcock helped to bring into being the powerful 'concert grand' with which we are now familiar. Babcock designed a layout of strings on two planes – the strings were arranged with one plane crossing over the other – and this made for greater sonority. Like William Stodart in London, he also adopted a cast-iron frame that made it possible to use heavier strings. This also made for more sonority.

By this time pianos were being produced in large numbers to accommodate a rapidly growing demand. Earlier, the daughters of the aristocracy and the rich merchant class had learned to play the harpsichord. With the extension of prosperity to a larger number of people in the first years of industrial expansion, the demand for music lessons spread. Girls were not encouraged to interest themselves in many activities in those days, but music was one that was permitted to them. Indeed, a girl of the middle or upper class who could not show some musical talent was considered as definitely inferior.

The popularity of the piano naturally increased the composer's opportunities.

One of the first musicians fully to perceive the revolutionary properties that lay within the piano was Muzio Clementi (1752–1832). Clementi, Italian born but English by adoption, had a piano showroom in London. His comprehensive studies, entitled *Gradus ad Parnassum*, clearly demonstrated the essentials of piano style and enabled pianists to acquire an adequate technique. *Gradus ad Parnassum*, as well as Clementi's fine sonatas and sonatinas (little sonatas), was widely used. Ludwig van Beethoven was only the most famous of those who found Clementi's technical studies indispensable.

Beethoven discovered how to express dramatic ideas and values through the piano. Other composers concentrated rather on the poetic qualities of piano tone. A young Irishman, John Field (1782–1837), worked for a time in Clementi's showroom demonstrating instruments to customers. A keen ear and a fertile imagination enabled

Field to emerge as a composer in his own right. Among other works, he wrote pieces supposedly inspired by night, which he termed *Nocturnés*. Of great charm in themselves, these pieces also inspired other composers. Frédéric Chopin (1810–69), was one of the great and original composers of piano music, and among his most poetic works were the *Nocturnes* in which he recollected some of the thoughts of John Field. Franz Liszt also praised Field and he too took note of the manner in which Field had achieved his most charming effects.

Mendelssohn and Schumann were among those who helped to popularize the piano, the former especially by *Songs without words*, the latter by his *Scenes of Childhood* and *Album for the Young*. This piano music was to be found in every drawing-room during the nineteenth century, and still belongs in the young pianist's repertoire. Both Mendelssohn and Schumann displayed the subtleties of the piano. Liszt, on the other hand, demonstrated its compelling power and brilliance. As a piano virtuoso Liszt dominated the concert-halls of Europe during his lifetime. Liszt's own compositions ranged widely from lyrical expression to vulgar exhibitionism. Behind him, however, there was always the shadow of a much greater figure, that of Beethoven, whose piano works Liszt's interpretation helped to make universally popular.

61 A reception for Franz Liszt, the great 19th-century pianist, in London in 1886; he is greeted by Joseph Joachim

18 Beethoven

LUDWIG VAN BEETHOVEN (1770–1827) was one of the really great creative artists in European civilization. His genius was acknowledged not only by musicians, but also by others, including those who were not remotely musical themselves. To many Beethoven represented, perhaps still does, the Romantic ideal of the composer.

At the beginning of this book it was established that musicians held a special place in society; and were also frequently regarded as being of a different order from other men. Today Beethoven is represented as a man whose qualities, defects, and genius were those of a unique personality.

In an age when people believed in, and looked for heroes, Beethoven was the artist cast in the mould of a hero. This is emphasized by many of the pictures and statues made in what was purported to be his likeness even after his death. During his lifetime Beethoven sought above all to fulfil his own destiny – to create what he wished to create – and by so doing to serve a humanity that in part he pitied and in part despised. Beethoven was angered by the lot of the majority of underprivileged people and by the ostentatious behaviour of the upperclass minority. He hated the divisions that existed in society. He despised the arrogance and frequent stupidity of the powerful. Above all, he rejected the idea that he should be told by others how to shape his thoughts and give vent to his ideas.

A creative genius to some extent grows out of material and spiritual forces that come together at a particular point in time. At the end of the eighteenth century, music had found many channels of expression, using various forms. It was the most popular and widespread of the arts and the one that best expressed at that time the views of the majority of sensitive people. Music at the same time combined the clarity that comes from logical thinking with the emotional warmth that stems from deep feeling.

The era of 'classical music' – in which music itself showed limitless possibilities – coincided with a period of intense revolutionary thought. Beethoven understood the significance of the classical on the one hand and the impulses of revolution on the other. Moreover, he understood the connection between the two. His understanding of the deeper issues of the time in which he lived was partly subconscious, but his intention to express them in a new and powerful manner was the consequence of deliberation.

Beethoven set out to make the sonata pattern, which came to him from C. P. E. Bach, Haydn, Mozart, and others, a comprehensive medium for expression through music. Through this he sought to proclaim both the achievements and the needs of humanity, and the rights and duties of the individual. Beethoven's music was imbued with a moral authority, and this is indicated by the manner in which his music has been accepted. It symbolized, and still symbolizes, the idea of freedom.

Beethoven was born in the German city of Bonn, on the River Rhine. His father was a musician on the staff of the Archbishop of Cologne. Beethoven's boyhood was anything but happy, for his father was often drunk and quarrelsome. Acquiring musical skills from the excellent musicians around him, however, the boy began to triumph over his disadvantages and to distinguish himself as a pianist and composer. He was inspired by the music of Bach (introduced to him by one of his teachers who had come west from Leipzig), Mozart, and Haydn, and he was aware of the forceful dramatic qualities shown by such composers as Luigi Cherubini (1760–1842), a Frenchman of Italian descent, and Etienne-Nicolas Méhul (1763–1817), who were active in France.

Encouraged by Haydn who first met him in Bonn, Beethoven later settled in Vienna. There he had lessons from a number of teachers, Haydn among them, and set about making his way in the world solely as a creative artist. Unlike his predecessors, Beethoven held no official appointment. He gave concerts, taught some pupils, and published his music where and when it was possible. His personality was vivid and vital, and if it was rough-spun (he spoke with a noticeable Rhineland accent) he nevertheless counted among his friends a number of rich, music-loving aristocrats. Their names appeared in the dedications of many of his works.

In Bonn, Beethoven had lived almost within earshot of the revolutionary happenings across the Rhine in France. He had hardly left Bonn for Vienna when the armies of Napoleon swept into the

62   Beethoven and the string quartet maintained by
Count Rasumovsky, Russian Ambassador in Vienna;
lithograph by A. Borckmann

Rhineland, to inspire the middle-aged with fear and the young with
hope. To the latter, the French invaders were messengers of a new
age, in which men should be freed from the restrictions and prejudices
that had hitherto prevailed. No lover of the established order, which
worked to the advantage of the rich, Beethoven made no secret of his
revolutionary thinking.

One of Beethoven's celebrated symphonies is the Third, in the key
of E flat, which has the meaningful title 'Eroica' ('heroic'). Composed
in 1804, this was to have been dedicated to Napoleon. But Napoleon's
acceptance of the title of 'Emperor' so infuriated Beethoven that he
withdrew the dedication, leaving only the general heading.

The 'heroic' ideal was at the centre of much of Beethoven's musical
thinking, and in one way or another the thinking of almost all his
successors in the nineteenth century. The 'heroic', however, was with
him a general rather than a particular view, and may be interpreted
as referring to the heroic qualities in all men. The climax of Beethoven's
symphonic career, which more or less covered the first quarter of the
nineteenth century, was the Ninth, or Choral, Symphony, of which

the final movement is a setting of Schiller's 'Ode to Joy'. Musically and emotionally it may be felt that all of Beethoven's symphonic works and concertos led to this great climax. Certainly Beethoven's contemporaries and those who came after him felt this to be the case. The Ninth Symphony was then, and still remains, one of the most meaningful works in the whole of music.

The same may be said of the Mass composed by Beethoven for the enthronement as Archbishop of the Archduke Rudolph, a friend of the composer. This work, the *Missa Solemnis* ('Solemn Mass') is too extensive and too difficult to be included in the general repertoire of purely Church music, but on that account is not to be considered as wholly secular. Rather it serves to break down the barriers that were felt to exist between sacred and secular art.

In a famous passage in this Mass, Beethoven gave emphasis to the prayer 'Give us peace', by prefacing it with the trumpets and drums that are associated with war. Beethoven's generation lived through a long period of war and this is reflected in many aspects of the art of the time. Apart from the obvious martial tone just referred to, and the symphony (not counted among the 'Nine') composed for Wellington's victory at the Battle of Victoria in 1812, all of Beethoven's music symbolizes the conflicts of the age in which he lived. It is more dramatic in rhythm than most previous music. It is richer and more varied in tone-colour. It is more extensive in scope. Beethoven took over the methods of Mozart and Haydn and extended them. He went back to the practices of J. S. Bach and incorporated them into his own mature style. Beethoven was a Classical composer, but the Romantic qualities of music are strongly evident in his works.

Earlier Classical masters more or less unconsciously reflected the world about them in their music. Beethoven did so deliberately. In the 'Pastoral' Symphony, he explored the relationship between man and nature that absorbed the attention also of many poets of that time (compare Schubert). In certain overtures ('Egmont' and 'Coriolanus') he tried to define the heroic virtues that make for greatness in men. In his one opera, *Fidelio*, he gave expression to man's desire for freedom and to the power of the love of man and woman.

Although Beethoven composed a few masterpieces of vocal music, he was pre-eminent as a creator of instrumental music. His chamber music – among which are sixteen string quartets, which represent the highest peak in this type of music – is the fulfilment of Classical intention, and the criterion by which later chamber music is judged. Belonging to the period in which the orchestra held a place of significance in its own right, Beethoven seized the opportunity offered. Beethoven's choral works, in their difficulty and immensity, reflected a large-scale development of secular choral societies. This development owed much to those who wished to perform the oratorios of Handel: works which made a deep impression on Mozart, Haydn, and Beethoven alike. Choral music was one means whereby musical experience was made available to the many. Beethoven's one oratorio, *The Mount of Olives*, and his Mass in C, were taken into the choral repertory at an early stage. Acceptance of the greater works came later.

A strange, solitary man, Beethoven never married. In his twenties he began to be afflicted with deafness. This increased until finally he was almost totally deaf and compelled to communicate to his friends through writing. Beethoven's manuscripts are among the most interesting of all that have come down from great musicians. They include many sketches which show the various stages through which his compositions passed before they reached their final form. They also include his 'conversation books', in which are incorporated his side of encounters with other people.

Beethoven prized his independence. He fought for this all his life. In so doing he fought for the right of free expression for all artists. He became the inspiration of all musicians in the Romantic era.

63   Music inspired many people seeking liberty after
the French Revolution. This is a group of Belgians
of Beethoven's time. His family originated in the
Flemish part of the country.

19 Songs and singing

BEETHOVEN WAS A GREAT MASTER of instrumental music. In his symphonies, concertos, and string quartets, he gave a general impression of the hopes and fears of many people at the beginning of the nineteenth century. Much of Beethoven's music cannot be described by words (although many have tried to do this) but in certain works he brought words and music close to each other. A notable example is the late String Quartet in A minor (Op. 132), in which the third movement is prefaced by the statement 'A sacred song of thanksgiving to God after recovery from illness, in the **Lydian** mode.' This is, as it were, a part-song without words, and wholly lyrical in character, for the note patterns are those of voice rather than of instrument.

During Beethoven's time poetry like music was changing. Three particular influences, all connected with one another, were at work. As in music, nature was one important factor. A love of nature stimulated a new respect for those who were thought to live closest to nature – the peasantry. From this came enthusiasm for folk-poetry and folk-music, and poets and musicians began to find merit in works composed in folk-song style. This was the second influence. The third influence on Romanticism was antiquity. What was old seemed to merit especial consideration. This was why Beethoven used the ancient 'Lydian' scale in his String Quartet in A minor.

The most popular poet who wrote in the folk-poetry idiom and in so doing created a new kind of folk-poetry was the Scotsman Robert Burns (1779–96), who also loved his country's music. Many German and Austrian poets cultivated a style that was closely related to the poetic styles of the people and of the past. Among these poets were Johann Wolfgang von Goethe (1749–1832), Ludwig Uhland (1787–1862), and Wilhelm Müller (1794–1827). There were many other poets in the German-speaking countries and their efforts to fashion a kind of poetry that was both evocative and full of feeling on the one hand, and simple and popular on the other, excited the interest of musicians.

In the eighteenth century the musical amateur who wished to sing for his own pleasure at home was not very well provided for. There was a great deal of opera music. There were elaborate cantatas. But the solo song – once cultivated to lute accompaniment – really had to await the popularization of the piano before it came into its own again. The piano was the ideal accompanying instrument since it was capable of so much response to the hands of a sensitive player.

The genius who put together all the patterns of thought that had formed themselves round the axis of words-with-music was Franz Schubert (1797–1828). Like Mozart, Haydn, and Beethoven, Schubert was associated with Vienna. Of these so-called 'Viennese' composers he was, indeed, the only one born there. Like Beethoven he determined that he would be a composer and only a composer. Like Beethoven he paid a heavy price for this determination, and his short life was unbelievably hard. He was supported by the goodwill of a few constant friends.

Whereas Beethoven concentrated on massive instrumental works, Schubert devoted the most part of his genius to composing songs. Schubert's melodies, often like the poems that inspired them, related to folk-song. These melodies, however, were sensitive to the pictorial elements in poetry and these he often treated with some freedom and in considerable detail in his piano accompaniments. Some of the finest of Schubert's songs are in the song-cycles *The beautiful girl at the mill*, and *Winter's journey*, and in the songs comprising these sets are many superb examples of colouring by means of piano figuration. The song-cycle, characterized by a common idea, became popular in the nineteenth century.

Schubert composed more than 600 songs, of which the most familiar are in the repertoire of almost every singer in the world. Two songs found their way into instrumental music, for 'The Trout' provided the theme for variation treatment in a quintet for strings and piano, while 'Death and the Maiden' served the same purpose in a string quartet. 'The Trout' is a song in which the picturesque accompaniment is the most immediately noticeable feature. 'Death and the Maiden' displays the wonderful emotional power of deep-set chords.

Schubert composed a considerable amount of chamber music and pianoforte music, and nine symphonies. Of these the Symphony in B minor was unfinished, and the last in C major lay undiscovered

64 *left* Jenny Lind, the 'Swedish Nightingale', was the best-paid singer of her time. A Berlin cartoonist suggests how well paid! *right* Jenny Lind singing in the Royal Opera House in Berlin

until Robert Schumann brought it to light in 1839. All Schubert's works are characterized by a lyrical spirit, that is by the spirit of song. In this way they contrast with the works of Beethoven whose main concern was less with the intrinsic qualities of melody (although, of course, he created many melodies which we may describe as 'beautiful') than with the development of germinal melodic ideas.

Many composers of the nineteenth century were interested in branches of art other than music. Because of the manner in which poetry had changed, because of the development of fiction, and because of the extension of interest in philosophy and politics, a large number were keen students of literature. Among Schubert's successors, both Robert Schumann (1810–56) and Richard Wagner (1813–83) were particularly well versed in literature, and both found new ways to give expression to literature through music. Schumann was a master of lyrical moods, Wagner of dramatic moods. The former distinguished himself through song, the latter through music-drama.

65 The Tripler Hall in New York was specially built for Jenny Lind

Schumann wrote more than 200 songs. They generally show a reflective and analytical quality and they often mirror the serious aspects of North German Romanticism. While the song was the centre of Schumann's musical extension, he added distinctive qualities to piano music. His wife, Clara (the daughter of a celebrated teacher, Frederick Wieck), was one of the best pianists of the nineteenth century, and much of Robert's music was inspired by her love for him and her belief in his genius.

Schumann was a master of the lyrical mood and this shows both in his songs and in his piano pieces. Like many other composers of the time he preferred shorter forms than that of the sonata.

Towards the end of his life Schumann came to appreciate the creative potential of a young man from Hamburg, Johannes Brahms (1833–97). The songs of Brahms are in the same tradition as those of Schumann and Schubert and maintain the lyrical impulse that was the main characteristic of the Romantic movement.

In the words of the greatest masters of the **Lied** there is a depth of purpose and meaning that reveals itself only after serious consideration.

Romantic song, associated with Romantic opera (*see* page 130), gave a new character to vocal music and encouraged a new style of singing. Before the full development of the *Lied*, those who wished to hear the finest singing went to the opera-house. In the nineteenth century the song recital came into vogue, and famous singers were able to accumulate large fortunes. One of the most celebrated singers of those days was the Swedish-born singer Jenny Lind (1820–87).

Jenny Lind sang in opera and in oratorio but she was able to fill a concert-hall with a programme of songs alone. In 1850, Jenny was invited to the United States, a tour having been arranged by Barnum the circus promoter. When she arrived in New York, two triumphal arches in her honour stood on the quayside, and 20,000 fans crowded the streets near her hotel. At midnight a chorus of 200, escorted by 300 city firemen, came to serenade the great singer.

The Tripler Hall was specially built for Jenny Lind's recitals. Barnum paid her $200,000 for the tour, and made a handsome profit. In Washington the President received her at the White House.

Twenty-two years before all this happened Franz Schubert, greatest of all composers of songs, had died in poverty.

66 Through modern media, 20th-century singers reach vast audiences

20 Music-drama

IN THE EIGHTEENTH CENTURY every ambitious young composer
hoped for the day when he would conquer the musical and fashionable world with an opera. In order to achieve this aim it was necessary
to compose a serious opera or a comic opera to an Italian libretto.
Italian had long been the international language of opera, the La
Scala Opera House in Milan was regarded as the greatest in the world,
and Italian composers had shown the world how to compose in a
manner congenial to singers and audiences alike. The Italian style of
singing, called **bel canto**, was indeed the basis of almost all vocal
melodic composition. But *bel canto*, however beautiful in design and
execution, often seemed to show little respect for the sense of words.

An opera, however, is a story. An opera in which the story is either
obscure or nonsensical is in the end an unsatisfactory work of art if
one believes that in an opera the arts of literature, music, and painting
should meet on more or less equal terms. Of course, not everyone
thinks (or thought) this, but during the Romantic period it became
an increasingly important consideration that opera should be
intelligible.

This was due to two factors. On the one hand the domination of
the world of opera by Italian musicians was resented by non-Italians.
On the other, in the years that followed the French Revolution, the
notion that the lives of people less exalted than kings and queens
(whether real or mythological) were fit subjects for artistic treatment
seemed both reasonable and attractive. Mozart and Beethoven had
demonstrated that operas of the first rank could be composed to
German words.

Mozart's *The Magic Flute* and Beethoven's *Fidelio* were landmarks
in history. The first because it raised the popular arts of pantomime
and *Singspiel* to the level of serious opera, and in so doing appeared to
lift the spirit of the German language and also of Germany itself. The
second was a landmark because it spoke eloquently of man's longing
for freedom.

In 1821 Carl Maria von Weber (1786–1826) went from Dresden

to Berlin for the first performance of his new opera *Der Freischütz*, a 'magic' opera based on an old German legend. Weber composed it at a time when young Germans were inspired by the sense of national pride that came after the defeat of the armies of Napoleon and the liberation of Germany. This sense of national pride embraced a love of the German past, of the countryside, of the traditions of city and village, and an idealistic faith in the qualities of the simple man – the peasant and the craftsman. This body of belief lay behind the German *Lied* and that it comes up again here shows how closely linked were song and opera in Germany. This can be appreciated in Weber's *Der Freischütz*, a study in good and evil, which is a blend of striking, often simple melodies, charming choruses, subtle instrumental colouring, and dramatic climaxes.

Der Freischütz is one of the most truly Romantic operas. With its sparkling melodies and original orchestration it is always a joy to hear and to see. In Germany it is the most performed of all native operas. Unlike many works of historical importance it was an immediate success, and this inspired many other German composers.

Composers who came in the wake of Weber included Heinrich Marschner (1795–1861), who composed some operas in the 'horror and mystery' manner, typical of one side of Romanticism; Albert Lortzing (1801–51), whose *The Czar and the Carpenter* is a warm-hearted comedy piece distinguished by its tunefulness; and Otto Nicolai's (1810–49) *The Merry Wives of Windsor*, a splendid representation of Shakespearian comedy in terms of music. The works of Lortzing and Nicolai in particular appealed strongly to the German middle class during the nineteenth century.

The greatest of Weber's followers, and one of the greatest of all composers, however, was Richard Wagner (1813–83). Wagner's lifetime spanned one of the most significant periods in German history, and he himself made a contribution to this history, and not only through his musical works.

Soon after Wagner's birth in Leipzig, the battle which led to the liberation of Germany from the domination of Napoleon was fought outside that city. Wagner grew up to believe in the strong liberal – even revolutionary – doctrines that were held by most educated young Germans in the early part of the nineteenth century. In 1848 he proclaimed himself a revolutionary and in the next year was among

67   Scene from a performance of *Der Freischütz* by the
Dresden State Opera

those in Dresden who attempted to overthrow the conservative
forces that were then in power. For this Wagner was expelled from
Germany for some years. The revolutionary, however, turned conservative. In later life Wagner supported the claims of the King of
Prussia and the war against France in 1870. In 1871 Wagner composed
a march to celebrate the founding of the German Empire. By now he
was, perhaps, the most talked about composer in the world. He was
also one of the most famous.

What a young musician needs is opportunity. One who wishes to
become a composer of operas needs an opera-house in which to work
and learn all the necessary techniques. In Italy and Germany there
were small theatres and opera-houses and the young composer, or
conductor, or singer, had more chance in those countries to serve a
satisfactory apprenticeship.

When he was young Wagner conducted in various unimportant
theatres. One of these was the charming little theatre at Bad Lauchstädt,
near Halle, which had been designed by Goethe and built some ten
years before Wagner's birth.

By 1842 Wagner had pushed ahead and in that year *The Flying
Dutchman* was performed in Dresden, where Weber had once been

Music Director. This opera – the tale of a seaman cursed to sail the seas for ever until redeemed by the love of a faithful woman – made a great impression, and the composer was appointed Music Director at Dresden, where he made many reforms. While still at Dresden, Wagner composed *Tannhäuser* and *Lohengrin*, which are both medieval stories in origin.

These operas were in a conventional style, in that they consisted of separate 'numbers', even though these were woven together with scenes. Wagner, however, believed that a new form of opera was required, one in which there should be as much unity of design as in a symphonic work. Indeed he set out to remodel opera with the symphonies of Beethoven as his inspiration. He worked intensively for twenty years before he could give to the world the complete *Ring of the Nibelungs*, a sequence of four 'music-dramas' based on old Nordic and German mythology. *The Ring* told of the doom of gods who lusted for power and were cursed by the spell of gold.

In 1857 Wagner composed *Tristan and Isolde*, a poignant love-story, and *The Mastersingers of Nürnberg*, a comedy based on life in a late medieval German city, and on its musical traditions. At the end of his life Wagner composed *Parsifal*, a religious drama.

In the last twenty years of his life Wagner was encouraged and supported by Ludwig II, King of Bavaria, whose preference for the arts to affairs of State, and for Richard Wagner to any of his Ministers, was the despair of his advisers. Due to this encouragement Wagner was able to achieve his life's ambition – a national theatre for music-drama. This was built at Bayreuth in Bavaria, and the theatre remains as a monument to a great musician.

Wagner not only created a new form of opera, but gave expression to a national mood. The new German music-drama was a symbol of the unity of the German nation, and also of the determination of its rulers to take a leading place in the affairs of the world.

The importance of music in national affairs is also illustrated by the career of Wagner's great contemporary, the Italian, Giuseppe Verdi (1813–1901). The son of an inn-keeper, Verdi was a born musician in a way that Wagner was not. That is to say, he had few skills or interests outside of music, to which he was trained from youth. Wagner, on the other hand, had studied many aspects of literature, history, art, and politics.

68   Walter and Eva, hero and heroine, and Hans
Sachs, of *The Mastersingers*; a modern Dresden
production

Verdi, however, shared with Wagner a deep love of his native land,
and he was especially happy when Italy became a united country
under a monarchy, in 1871. During the years in which Italians, under
the leadership of Giuseppe Garibaldi (1807–82), strove for unification
of the separate Italian states, the operas of Verdi became popular
symbols of the desire of Italians to unite.

Verdi was one of the great masters of melody and in this respect his
operas maintain the traditions established in Italy during the seventeenth century. He also had a powerful instinct for dramatic expression
in music which showed itself not only in melodic outline but also in
telling, often unexpected, harmonic effects and brilliant orchestration.

Verdi came into prominence, as did Wagner, in 1842, when his
Nabucco (Nebuchadnezzar) was produced at La Scala Opera House in
Milan. This opera is known to many who may be unaware of its name
through the superb 'Prisoners' Chorus'. Verdi's tunes, the richness
and immediate appeal of his instrumentation, and the exciting
character of his operas made him popular throughout Italy. In Paris
and London, audiences withheld at first their acclaim. Indeed, in the
French capital where the 'grand operas' of Gioacchino Rossini (1792–
1868) were most popular, the critics were sometimes scathing about
Verdi's 'vulgarity'.

But Verdi knew his own people and he continued to develop along the lines established in Italy. However, his wide range of subjects and his gift for dramatic expression made his works irresistible. The most celebrated of Verdi's operas are *Il Trovatore*, *La Traviata*, *Aida*, and *Otello*.

Il Trovatore was based on a Spanish story. *La Traviata*, an opera treating of a contemporary subject rather than one that was historical, was based on a novel by Alexandre Dumas (1824–95). *Aida* was commissioned to celebrate the opening of the Suez Canal and was first performed in Cairo in 1871. *Otello*, the tragedy from Shakespeare, was produced when the composer was seventy-four years old. Six years later he produced his last opera, *Falstaff*, and the performance was the occasion of a great demonstration of appreciation for the composer.

The works of Verdi and Wagner were complementary. Verdi summed up the great Italian tradition of melody and vocal beauty. His music appeals to the emotions. Wagner's music, more contrapuntal in texture, and bound up with philosophic and literary ideas, could only have come into being in a German context. Verdi spoke eloquently and literally to the man-in-the-street; his tunes were played by organ-grinders in cities far distant from his native Italy. Wagner's eloquence was combined with argument and his attitude was less that of a minstrel than that of a prophet.

Verdi and Wagner were great composers, but they were more than composers. For each was a national symbol. And in the age in which they lived nationalism was the most powerful and most emotive force.

69   In Paris in the mid-19th century opera fans were often rowdy. The quarrel here is between supporters of Verdi and Rossini

21 National styles of music

MUSIC, IT IS OFTEN SAID, is a 'universal language'. Up to a point it is – but only up to a point. It depends on what people are accustomed to. In the Western world musicians and their audiences have learned to find meaning in arrangements of sounds and sonorities that have been developed through international co-operation – undertaken sometimes willingly and sometimes unwillingly.

This kind of music, often wrongly termed 'classical music', has hitherto been peculiar to the Western world. It grew out of particular experiences and social organizations and was without significance in other parts of the world until Western trade and Western manners in general began to extend their influence.

At the present time East and West have begun to share musical experiences, so that while the classical music of Europe is now played in Japan and China, the classical music of India is increasingly performed and admired in the West. That this is so is due less to the concern of musicians for exploring far afield, than to the ever-increasing conquest of time and space that makes the world a much smaller place than it was.

In the period of the Renaissance, Europe took its cultural lead from the Italian States, and was content to do so. For a disunited Italy was politically weak and supremacy in the arts did not appear as a political threat to anyone. Thus Italy became the first training-ground of musicians competent to direct and advise the aristocratic and ecclesiastical patrons of music all over the Western countries of Europe.

Somewhat later Italy was overtaken by Germany. By the nineteenth century, students from many countries went to study in the conservatories of Germany, hoping to imbibe something of the spirit of the great German masters.

Teachers in Leipzig and other cities offered assurance that the 'rules' of music that had been deduced from the practice of J. S. Bach on the one hand and of the symphonic masters on the other were a guarantee of excellence. There was no doubt at all in their minds that it was their duty to teach students to compose in the 'German manner'.

The two giants of nineteenth-century music, as has been seen, were Verdi and Wagner. Their achievements helped to evoke and fulfil the hopes of national unity in their respective countries. But nationalism at that time was a powerful force in other lands as well, and as it gathered strength, began to create new attitudes to musical expression in many places.

In Italy, Germany, and Austria, musical traditions and institutions were so strong, and music so much a part of general experience, that there was no compelling reason to appeal to a separate folk-song tradition (in spite of this the folk-music influence was strong). In countries where there was not a distinctive indigenous musical style, however, it seemed to be necessary to establish musical independence by relating to native folk-song tradition.

Folk-song belonged to the larger movement towards independence. It was the voice of the ordinary people who constituted the main body of a nation. This was particularly the case in the Eastern countries of Europe, where a ruling aristocratic class, regarding folk-music as merely barbaric, trained its musical sights on Milan, Vienna, Leipzig, or Berlin. In due course something similar happened in the United States, where the music of the most oppressed members of the land was represented by the Negro spiritual and the 'blues'. These were to create a new style of music in the course of time – one which held a universal cry of protest. But the official musicians for long continued to look abroad for inspiration and instruction.

In many countries there was another factor to be taken into consideration. Small nations which had once developed their own traditions lost the opportunity to continue to do this when they came under the control of larger neighbours, and their individual languages were forced into obscurity. In Britain the ancient Celtic languages, in eastern Europe the Magyar and Slavonic languages, were relegated to subordinate status. But in the nineteenth century poets, musicians, and all who wished for a liberation of the human spirit, saw that these languages held a beauty and significance of their own. The living tradition of a language was that to be found in folk-song.

Protest in music went along with some tendencies in the main musical traditions, just as it went against others. Beethoven, Weber, and Wagner symbolized new ideals, and by daring techniques and originality of expression, stimulated other composers to develop more colourful means of romantic and dramatic statement. Franz Liszt gave additional impetus with his development of a narrative style in the symphonic poem. Liszt offered other incentives as well. He was a Hungarian and proud of his birthright, and of the music that was to be heard in the Hungarian countryside. He was most of all inspired by the vivid rhythms of the age-old dances of the Magyar people, by the moving character of folk-songs often lavishly and beautifully embellished, and by the brilliant instrumental sonorities of the gipsy musicians. On all of this the symphonic poem *Hungaria* (1856) is a fine commentary.

Liszt knew the gipsies who lived near the Neusiedler Lake. Long before, Josef Haydn had known the ancestors of these same gipsies, and he too had introduced musical ideas from their environment into his symphonies and string quartets. The practice of introducing quotations from folk-music into art music was very old. But the belief that folk-music was as significant as art music, and its values of equal worth, was something new.

On all sides composers began to protest against indignities to their national pride. Michael Glinka (1803–57), angry that French and Italian influences prevailed in the musical life of St Petersburg, determined that Russians should have their own musical expression. After travelling through many countries Glinka wrote how 'home sickness awakened in me the thought to compose in a Russian manner, and the idea of a Russian national music became stronger and stronger'. In 1836 Glinka's opera *Ivan Sussanin* – at the Tsar's request renamed *A Life for the Czar* – was produced in St Petersburg. This opera, with Russian and Polish folk-tunes and patriotic choruses, became a rallying-point for young patriots and intellectuals. The final chorus, 'Praise to thee, my Russian fatherland', was a great inspiration, not only to Russians, but also to many Slavonic musicians. In 1842 Glinka's *Russlan and Ludmilla*, a fairy opera based on a poem by Alexander Pushkin (1799–1837), was performed for the first time. The overture to this opera is a popular item in the orchestral repertoire today and exemplifies the brilliant and direct manner of the musical expression of its composer.

Glinka inspired a group of Russian composers, among whom were

70   Wagner monument near Dresden, where the composer directed at the Royal Opera from 1842 to 1849

71   Memorial to Chopin in Warsaw

Mily Balakirev (1837–1910), and César Cui (1835–1918).

Cui was half-French, half-Russian, his father having been a French officer who remained behind after the Napoleonic invasion of Russia. In Poland, the case of musical nationalism was first promoted by Frédéric Chopin, who was also half-French. His father was a French resident in Poland.

Chopin composed many works which were based on the rhythms of national dances, the most familiar being the **polonaise** and the **mazurka**.

In 1848, Europe was convulsed with outbreaks of revolution. The temper of the times was similar to that of our own day, except that whereas in the nineteenth century it was 'national rights' that caused demonstrations and revolutions it is now 'civil rights'.

Modern revolutionary thought has its own music – the 'protest song' being universally familiar. In the last century the protest song was more often than not wrapped up within an opera. Two of the most famous of nineteenth-century folk-operas were *Halka*, by Stanislav Moniuszko (1819–72), and *The Bartered Bride*, by Bedřich Smetana (1824–84). The one was Polish, the other Czech. Both works showed aspects of national life and embraced national melodies. *Halka* was a tragedy, *The Bartered Bride* a comedy; but both were intended to achieve the same end. Moniuszko and Smetana, living through times of trial but also hope, tried to draw the attention of their countrymen to their own traditions and to their responsibilities as patriots.

The most celebrated nationalistic composer of the nineteenth century was Antonin Dvořák (1841–1904). Coming from a Bohemian peasant background he knew the innermost secrets and strength of national life. He learned how to unite the impulses of folk-dance and folk-song with the conventions of classical music and in so doing was able to command the attention of the whole musical world. He composed works of every kind: symphonies, concertos, songs, oratorios, chamber music, and operas, in all of which traits of Bohemian folk-music are recognizable.

Dvořák's distinctive style won acclaim in many countries. He was a welcome visitor in England and the United States. He lived for a time in North America, and showed clearly his respect for the music of the Negroes. He said that this should form the basis of a national music in the United States, and in his most famous symphony – 'From the New World' – he included melodies that seemed to have their origins in Negro music.

In 1893 a World's Fair was held in Chicago. Music was an important part of this occasion and many national groups organized characteristic musical events. Dvořák was present on 'Czech Day' to conduct some of his own music. There was also a good deal of Welsh music to be heard during the World's Fair, for an 'International Eisteddfod' was organized. This followed the pattern of the national Welsh Eisteddfod that was revived in the nineteenth century.

Nationalism helped to break down the influence of the Great Powers in music. It made people in many lands investigate their own traditions and examine the hidden reserves of culture. It also encouraged the development of musical education, with emphasis on national music. The cause of nationalism was protected most zealously in those countries where national independence barely existed. The most notable and effective studies of national music have been made in the Eastern countries of Europe, where the Hungarians – Zoltán Kodály (1872–1967), scholar and composer, and Béla Bartók (1881–1945) – exerting a strong influence, may be seen to have brought one side of the work of Liszt to fulfilment.

22 Music and painting

ART IN ALL ITS MANY FORMS arises from man's emotional responses to people and to situations. The basis of art, then, may be seen as joy or sorrow, hope or fear, or any of an infinite number of states that lie within these points. It is often said that the artist seems to be searching for beauty. This, however, is nothing more nor less than the search for order out of disorder; for peace out of conflict. The artist looks for special answers to difficult questions, and the questions are those that we all ask.

At one extreme, art may seem to be informative. This is the condition of many kinds of literary expression. At the other extreme, art may appear to be almost entirely **abstract**, with no obvious point of contact with what are considered the realities of existence. Perhaps the principle of abstractions can best be understood by listening to some kinds of music and by looking at certain kinds of sculpture.

Between these extremes there is an almost infinite variety of expression, and continual change. Because of development in techniques, the arts change within themselves, but they also change in relationship with each other. Sometimes, therefore, we discover music being kept at a distance from literature. In the Classical period (or afterwards in the Classical manner) when a composer wrote a symphony it was as a rule free of any kind of verbal narrative interest, while in an aria a composer often seemed more intent on spinning notes for a singer than on making sense of the words. In the nineteenth century, on the other hand, orchestral music, in the shape of symphonic poem, or tone poem, set out to illustrate stories in some detail.

After Berlioz, a most conspicuous pioneer of narrative music, there was Franz Liszt, and his ambitious tone poems stimulated many other composers to try to do what music does not readily do; that is, without words to give information that can really only be conveyed through words. The later masters of **programme music**, making use of the lavish instrumental resources opened up to them by Berlioz, Liszt, and Wagner, designed works that satisfied the wishes of audiences that filled the many concert-halls built during the

72   Abstract composition by sculptor Lajos Barta

nineteenth century.

Programme music – the stories written out in accompanying programme books – covered the philosophic and psychological territory
marked out by the plays of Shakespeare, the poems of Byron, and
Goethe's *Faust*. Programme music embraced popular themes from
fictional literature, and absorbed heroic ideals. Programme music also
admirably met some of the requirements of musical nationalists. To
this day programme music occupies a prominent place in the concert
repertoire, because many people are reluctant to give up the idea that
music is concerned with story-telling.

There are many famous examples of Late Romantic programme
music. They include *My Country* by Smetana, *Romeo and Juliet* by
Peter Ilyich Tchaikovsky (1840–93), *Falstaff* by Edward Elgar (1857–

1934), *Don Quixote* and *Don Juan* by Richard Strauss (1864–1949), and *Finlandia* by Jean Sibelius (1865–1951). Narrative invaded other kinds of music too. Symphonies in the grand narrative manner culminated in such works as the 'Pathetic' Symphony by Tchaikovsky and the ambitious and detailed symphonies of Gustav Mahler (1860–1911).

During the nineteenth century, size in itself appeared to have some special virtue. There was a general inflation of all the arts, exemplified in vast, often ugly, public buildings, and in musical works designed for great forces of performers. Before the nineteenth century was over, however, a reaction set in. It was felt by some that the story-telling function of music could be discontinued and that music could renew itself by relating to new trends in painting.

Claude Debussy (1862–1918), was one of the most original composers of modern times, and one of the pioneers of contemporary attitudes within musical expression. Debussy was deeply sensitive to painting and to every visual symbol. The effects of light and shade, the continual interplay of colours in nature, and the way in which these were expressed by a number of French painters of his time fascinated him. The Impressionist manner of Claude Monet (1840–1926) and Edouard Manet (1823–83) and other painters, represented a desire to capture the transient effects of nature. Impressionist painting was lighter, more restrained, less concerned with the seeming permanence of objects than the kind of painting which had hitherto been fashionable, and Debussy managed to translate the feeling of such painting into music.

This, after all, was not too difficult. The Impressionist painters attempted to suggest *movement* through colour. The Impressionist composer, while reacting against the 'bigness' of Romantic music, tried to suggest colour through *movement*.

Debussy simplified some musical conventions and encouraged younger musicians to be less obedient to the so-called 'rules' of harmony, and form, and so on. He encouraged composers to trust their ears and to seek out fresh experiences. Debussy listened to the overtones of bells, to the sounds of nature, to the instrumentation of Oriental music, and the sound patterns of pre-Classical European music. He brought back ideas that had once been in vogue but long forgotten. He also taught that economy is a virtue; that a composer should decide how few sounds he needs rather than how many, that he should explore the edges of silence.

Debussy's most famous orchestral work is *L'Après-midi d'un faune* (The Afternoon of a Faun), and this typifies the new approach. Debussy was a master of piano music and he composed songs and chamber music of striking beauty. His opera *Pelléas et Mélisande*, a 'lyrical drama', is one of the masterpieces of modern times and quite at the opposite extreme from 'realistic' drama. When first performed in 1902 *Pelléas et Mélisande* was regarded as problematic and was abused by conservative Parisians. Sixty years later, in the Debussy centenary year, it was performed in Vienna, Hamburg, Berlin, Glyndebourne (England), and Paris, in recognition of its being one of the greatest works of the twentieth-century theatre.

Movement in music has been a source of inspiration to painters and sculptors from the earliest times. In France the affection of painters for the sister art has been especially notable. Some of the most musical of drawings and paintings were those of Hilaire-Germain-Edgar Degas (1834–1917), whose friendship with the composer Ludovic Halévy, enabled him to visit the Paris Opera freely. The most striking reflection of music in terms of line and colour in French art, however, is in the works of Raoul Dufy (1877–1953). Dufy, friend of the conductor Charles Munch, and the cellist Pau Casals (1876–1973), with Mozart as one of the most profound influences on his life, has interpreted countless facets of musical activity with an almost unique sense of precision. Among his works are a series of *Homages*: to Mozart, to Bach, and to Debussy. On a famous painting, *The Red Violin*, Dufy inscribed on a pictured page of music behind the violin, 'Music and painting by Raoul Dufy.' That was to show how close music and painting can be.

Many aspects of twentieth-century art show affinities with music. The geometry of abstract music is reflected in the art of Wassily Kandinsky (1866–1944) and Paul Klee (1879–1940). The American artist, Thomas Wilfred, made an astonishing visual realization of sonata form in his *Lumia Suite. Op. 158* (Museum of Modern Art, New York). More recently the young German painter and composer, Horst Loewel, has not only expressed his response to musical works through paintings but also invented electronic music to comment on the paintings.

23 The continuing tradition

THE HISTORY OF MUSIC is partly a record of revolutions which have been made respectable. The same process may be observed in other fields of human endeavour. No doubt the most revolutionary figure in the music of modern times – because his ideas were effective across a wide expanse of experience – was Beethoven. But a generation after his death Beethoven was safely embalmed among the 'immortals', and his works apparently had become the undisputed property of the middle class. Somewhat later the music-drama of Wagner went the same way.

Concert-halls and opera-houses built during the latter part of the nineteenth and the first part of the twentieth centuries were designed more or less exclusively for the use of the more conforming members of the middle class. It was suspected by the irreverent that many people attended concerts and operas only in order to be seen.

It has already been noticed, however, that musical nationalists were presenting ideas that were in conflict with many established principles. But for the most part even the most nationally minded nineteenth-century composers found it expedient ultimately to arrive at a compromise. So it is that the element of nationalism within the music of, say, Dvořák, now seems to most people to be of not much more than passing interest. That is because the element of nationalism is wrapped up within the acceptable conventions of nineteenth-century musical expression.

Dvořák was much indebted to Johannes Brahms (1833–97), who wielded considerable influence in Vienna when Dvořák was at the beginning of his career. Although Czech by birth, Dvořák was a citizen of the Austrian Empire, since his native Bohemia was part of that empire. It was therefore necessary for him to establish a reputation in the capital city of the empire.

Brahms, who was born in Hamburg, was brought into prominence when his early works won the warm approval of Robert and Clara Schumann. He came to be regarded as a worthy exponent of the great traditions of German music. His position in this respect became more assured when, together with his friend Joseph Joachim (1871–1907), the virtuoso violinist and composer, he took a stand against the then 'modern' music of Wagner and Liszt. That controversy has long since been forgotten. Even so there are those today who still see Brahms's music in opposition to that of Wagner and Liszt. The reason is simple. Brahms wrote symphonic music but no music-dramas. Wagner wrote no symphonic music but almost exclusively music-dramas. Brahms wrote abstract, or absolute, music; Liszt wrote programme music.

That statement is no doubt too simple; for now, looking back, we may be more aware of the over-all nineteenth-century character of the music of nineteenth-century musicians than of the distinctions separating them.

Brahms composed four symphonies, two piano concertos, one violin concerto, one double concerto for violin and violoncello, and much pianoforte and chamber music. The major works were designed according to the principles enunciated by Beethoven in his symphonic works. After some initial doubt, Brahms's orchestral music was accepted as being 'Classical' and by the time he was fifty he was listed with Mozart, Haydn, and Beethoven, as a great Classical master.

During the nineteenth century the music critic began to exercise a great deal of influence. Edouard Hanslick (1825–1904), one of the most respected critics of those days, spared no pains to promote the cause of Brahms, whom he regarded as the great master of symphony and heir to the great tradition. Brahms was further helped by Hans Richter (1843–1916), the eminent conductor who was of the same opinion. To Hanslick and Richter, aware of the great musical traditions of Vienna where their own activities were centred, it seemed only right that Brahms's name should be put on the list of the 'Viennese classics'.

The popularity of Brahms remains (at least in the German-speaking and English-speaking countries) and his symphonic works, their occasional austerity relieved by beautiful, nostalgic, melodic lines, appear as monuments of high thinking and social stability.

The form of the symphony was the subject of much discussion in the nineteenth century. The young composer, no matter what his country, was then, and for some time to come, made to understand that in order to establish a reputation for competence (if not for genius) it was obligatory to write a symphony.

The backyard of music is strewn with unsuccessful symphonies. Among those that dropped out of the running at an early stage were the symphonies and/or concertos of Hermann Goetz (1840–76), Arthur Sullivan (1842–1900), Camille Saint-Saëns (1835–1921), and Julius Röntgen (1855–1932). One of the reasons for a long casualty list of symphonic works was the narrowing of opportunity that occurred paradoxically with the greatest expansion of symphony orchestras.

When Wagner lived in Munich, the Director of Music there was Hans von Bülow (1830–94), whose skills as orchestral conductor made people aware not only of the qualities of Wagner's scores but also of the necessity for modern music to be interpreted by a specialist. Hans Richter was also a famous Wagner conductor, but both he and von Bülow built up a large repertoire of works and as their fame spread they undertook conducting engagements in many parts of the world. From the time of von Bülow and Richter, the conductor occupied a dominant role. Richter was Hungarian by birth, and so was the next notable founding-father of the conductor's art. This was Arthur Nikisch (1855–1922), who was particularly associated with Leipzig, but well known from Budapest to Boston.

In the course of time the conductor's reputation depended not on his ability to keep orchestral players in order but on his 'interpretation'. Audiences, much the same the world over, came to prefer interpretations of symphonies with which they were familiar to interpretations of those which were unfamiliar. In this way the symphonic field, so far as the general public was concerned, began to contract.

Dvořák, however, partly because his works were praised by Brahms, was admitted to the symphonic sphere, and his stature has grown with the realization that his freshness, exuberance, and perception of beauty in sound derive from a respectable symphonic ancestry that was to some extent independent. The symphonies of Tchaikovsky made a great impression at the end of the nineteenth century, and were readily accepted by audiences, who found their highly emotional content a mirror of their own perplexities and conflicts.

The symphonies of Gustav Mahler (1860–1911), and of Anton Bruckner (1842–96), have taken longer to find acceptance. At one time they too were considered too obviously emotional and descriptive, to qualify as 'abstract' music. Now, towards the end of the twentieth century, the emotional content of music does not disqualify it so far as the new, less inhibited younger audiences of the present day are concerned. Mahler, who was a great conductor and opera director as well as composer, suffered in his youth from the hostility of Brahms and his supporters. Bruckner, who was also an Austrian but who never occupied positions of importance, was another victim of Brahms's disapproval. Bruckner's crime was to have admired Wagner and to have built Wagnerian principles into his symphonic structures.

The influence that Brahms wielded is also shown by the respect paid to his music by Jean Sibelius and Edward Elgar. Sibelius went to Vienna as a student in the hope (which turned out to be a vain hope) of being able to work with Brahms. Elgar regarded Brahms's Third Symphony in F minor as one of the great examples of symphonic art. He gave lectures on the structure of this work, which he also often conducted with the London Symphony Orchestra.

The two symphonies of Elgar, as well as the Violin Concerto, brought English music firmly into the international field of music. For these works, as well as *The Dream of Gerontius* and the *Enigma Variations*, were played in Europe and the United States in the first decade of this century. Sibelius was and remains the sole representative of Finland in symphony, and his seven works in this genre have a Northern reserve that gives them what is taken to be a 'Finnish' character.

The Brahms influence may thus be seen to run through the designs of composers of many schools, and it is a lasting influence.

73   Munich, 1865: von Bülow conducts the first performance of Wagner's *Tristan and Isolde*

24 Survival and revival of old values

WESTERN MUSICAL TRADITION is a sensitive and complex organism. Looked at from the outside – that is from either a primitive, or an Oriental point of view – this tradition is a unified whole, but unified because it all seems incomprehensible. The same, of course, applies the other way round, so that to many Western ears Eastern music is monotonous and without meaning.

The complexity and sensitivity of the Western tradition have depended on the interrelationship of certain basic concepts and techniques.

Music has melodic, rhythmic, harmonic, and tone-colour properties. To the extent that music is organized sound we could discover music if only one of these properties were evident. Normally, however, music is the consequence of all of the properties being present, but each element subjected to different emphasis. Melody, rhythm, harmony, and tone-colour, however, are in themselves complex in organization, the degree of complexity being due to the creative attitude in a particular instance. The artist in any medium is never isolated. He relies to a great extent on the ideas generated in his environment.

This means that when an experienced listener hears a musical work with which he is not familiar, he can ascribe it to a period, even sometimes to a composer. Where the listener hears one kind of pattern of melodies, within one kind of sequence of pieces, and assigned to one kind of instrumental ensemble, he recognizes, for example, a Baroque idiom. Another set of dispositions gives a Classical idiom. And so on.

In spite of experience the listener can, however, arrive at the wrong answer, for composers do not always work out their thoughts as we expect from their previous work.

In the previous chapter the symphonic tradition was described as being a continuous, evolutionary, process – which in one way it is. Its continuity may seem to come from each composer looking back from today to yesterday and carefully continuing from that point.

But sometimes the imaginative composer wonders what music

would be like if what was in vogue not yesterday but the day before yesterday, or the day before that, were taken into consideration.

In the Classical period – or still under the shadow of the Classical period – some composers looked sideways and explored folk-song. Some looked backwards and explored possibilities that had not been examined too closely for some time.

What we now call Baroque music was once regarded as dry and unimaginative. The truth then dawned that the Baroque style had many virtues, that it led to work that could hardly be described as unimaginative.

The style of Bach was idealized during the second part of the nine-teenth century. All kinds of composers – Beethoven, Mendelssohn, Schumann, Liszt, among them – composed preludes and fugues to denote a keenness for the Bach idiom. Brahms composed motets which really do sound Bach-like in intensity of feeling and energy of counterpoint. The last movement of his Fourth Symphony is a **passacaglia**, and once again the character is thoroughly Baroque.

Renewal of the Baroque spirit seemed one way out of the impasse at which music had arrived. Towards the end of the last century it was felt that all that could be composed in the conventional styles had already been done. To some extent Brahms reversed the signposts, but he was too strongly symphonic and Romantic in outlook to persuade his more enthusiastic disciples to tread the backward road.

A conspicuous traveller on this road was the German composer Max Reger (1873–1916). Reger composed a great deal of music, much of it – including some beautiful songs and orchestral suites and variations – thoroughly warm and Romantic. But in looking for means to enrich Romanticism by reference to the past he broke right through the Romantic barriers. In his passacaglias, fugues, fantasias, and chorale preludes (many of these works written for the organ) Reger showed that modern ideas could indeed be incorporated within old and relatively strict forms.

Reger has never enjoyed the reputation outside of Germany that he has in his own country. Nevertheless, his intense study of Baroque method and the accumulation of scholars round this area of music, have exerted considerable influence on twentieth-century music.

Paul Hindemith (1895–1963), was a German composer too, and the methods of Baroque expression are evident in all his instru-

74 A modern harpsichord, played here by
Herbert Collum

mental works, where the structure of music shows an endless capacity
for weaving contrapuntal patterns. Counterpoint means interesting
melodic lines throughout musical texture. A contrapuntal style, therefore, was thought to be ideal for amateur groups of players, for this
would allow every performer an opportunity to participate. Hindemith was one of the foremost twentieth-century composers who
seriously considered the needs of amateur musicians. So too was
Ralph Vaughan Williams, whose strength of expression derives in
large part from the Baroque patterns in his scores.

The Fourth Symphony of Vaughan Williams ends with a stern and
dissonant fugue. The Fifth Symphony ends with a serene passacaglia. Vaughan Williams, however, looked farther back than the
Late Baroque and he was greatly influenced by the choral music of
the great English composers of the sixteenth century. This is shown
in Vaughan Williams's best-known work, the *Fantasia on a Theme of
Thomas Tallis*, for string quartet and double string orchestra.

The attention paid to music of the past is one of the more remarkable features of modern musical life. Every conductor of old music
who wishes to do his job properly aims at an 'authentic performance'.

This means getting as near as possible to the original score, tone-colours, manner of interpretation, and so on. So we have old instruments restored to popularity, among which the recorder and the harpsichord are notable examples.

A composer is affected by developments of this sort whether he wishes to be or not. Thus we find recorders and harpsichords restored to musical experience not only through scholarly revival of old music, but also in new music. The harpsichord, like the organ (although **electronic** in this case), turns up in popular music where its 'Baroqueness' is less important than the tingling effect of its sonorities.

A composer who uses many Baroque devices is often described as 'neo-Baroque'. If we are allowed neo-one-thing then we must be allowed neo-another. It is not surprising therefore that we may also discover 'neo-Classicism' as a factor in modern musical experience.

Classical music was based on the principle of orderliness, and more especially on the orderly balance of key-centres. The great apostle of order in music in the middle years of the twentieth century was Igor Stravinsky (1882–1971), whose belief in the worth of Classical principles in general was proclaimed both through musical works and through speeches and writings.

The most distinctively neo-Classical work of the twentieth century in that its origins are most obvious to the ordinary music-lover, is the *Classical Symphony* of Sergei Prokofiev (1891–1953). This is not only a defence of orderliness in music, however, but also a gentle caricature of primness. One can, Prokofiev suggests, look back, but one cannot turn back.

In the United States the place of the Classical spirit in contemporary musical thought has been argued particularly by the composer and teacher Roger Sessions (b. 1896). Adherence to Classical principle is not, he says, a matter of using Classical forms, but of 'experiencing anew certain laws which are inherent in the nature of music itself'. That takes us back to the underlying concept of abstract art; that it is itself and nothing else and unconnected to and uninfluenced by the rest of the world.

There is, of course, a quite contrary argument: that nothing is abstract, and that everything must relate to something.

25 Twentieth-century revolution

AT THE BEGINNING of the twentieth century, most music-lovers in the Western world – the patrons of concert-halls and opera-houses, and amateur players and singers – thought they knew precisely where they stood. Music, they believed, was divided into various categories, according to scope and usage. It was intended primarily to give pleasure. The best of it had been composed in the past, and if by chance any musical works belonged to the present, they observed well-established rules. Above all, music was not intended to provoke uneasiness. The composer was no more than an entertainer they said.

This tranquil musical scene was an illusion. In some quarters, perhaps, the illusion still persists. Today, however, music is in no sense what it was thought to be only a few years ago. The great difference between now and then is that music-lovers and some musicians have a more catholic outlook. Popular music, in short, is

75 (*above*) Oberlin College, Ohio, Conservatory of Music, designed by Japanese architect Yamasaki

not pushed out of sight as though it carried noxious vapours. It is heard and often esteemed for what it is – one of the foundations of musical experience.

At the beginning of this century music which 'obeyed the rules' of harmony, counterpoint, and so on, was thought to be 'good' music. Such music was approved by authorities in music-schools and by many other people as well. Debussy in particular realized that ideas based on authoritarian principles were wrong and that fresh thoughts were due on the nature of music.

First of all the tonal system on which Western Classical music was based was, it seemed, worn-out. Debussy revived some of the scales or modes used in the Middle Ages and also in folk-song, and he made frequent use of a scale without half-tones and known, therefore, as the **whole-tone scale**. The result of introducing these systems was to inaugurate new thinking about harmonies. The old note-groups, or chords, created from the major and minor scales that had served as the basis of expression for almost 300 years would no longer work. Debussy's harmonies were intuitive and impressionist, and subject to the nature of a particular mood rather than to fixed 'rules of harmony'.

After Debussy reduced the significance of conventional tonal theories the way was open for composers who considered that **atonality** was not only not objectionable but positively desirable. The first composer to dispense boldly with tonal procedures was Arnold Schoenberg (1874–1951), a Viennese musician, who was closely associated with a group of painters intent on developing new modes of expression and new principles. Wassily Kandinsky and Paul Klee (*see* page 144), and Franz Marc (1880–1916), were important members of the artistic group whose works are economical, abstract, and experimental. 'It is better', said Marc, 'to make a tradition and not just to live off one.' That is what Schoenberg did. He created a tradition. A first step was to dismantle the old tonal system entirely. So that Schoenberg's name was first linked with atonality. At the same time, if less conspicuous, other composers began to move in the same direction. Among them was the American Charles Ives (1874–1954).

Tonality is only one part of music. In the wake of the Baroque, Classical, and Romantic eras, however, tonal procedures sometimes became a kind of obsession. That obsession was removed bit by bit. The first signs of change were evident on the eve of the First World War, when every institution was on the point of upheaval. That helps to explain how innovations within music were part of other processes of change and also why they followed one another with great rapidity.

The most vital part of music is rhythm, and the more rhythmic musical expression seems the more physical is its character. In the nineteenth century Beethoven impressed his character on musical thought at least in part by powerful, urgent, rhythmic impulses that to some people appeared to be almost primitive. Twentieth-century music in its broadest aspects has been dominated more by rhythmic factors than by any other. Rhythms from folk-music became more insistent during the development of the nationalist idioms, culminating in the early ballets of Stravinsky and the powerful Hungarian impulses of Zoltán Kodály and Béla Bartók. But the most insistent rhythms of all have come from the music of the American Negroes, by way of jazz, in New Orleans and Chicago.

Jazz was the music of the underprivileged and in the hands of many artists achieved a dignity and depth of its own. Coming from the religious intensity of the Negro slaves and from their piercing vision of a new world, jazz brought back to music a renewed sense of social purpose and helped to make people aware of human needs. The jazz musician is impelled towards creativity by his responses to the world. His art is notable for the richness of its rhythmic and instrumental colouring and for the great part played in it by improvisation.

It is clear that fundamental changes of one sort in an art involve other changes. The tonal and rhythmic changes detailed were, of course, not isolated. Once the tonal and rhythmic factors of musical expression were changed, then other changes followed.

Each age enjoys its own range of colour stimulation. In music tone-colour is partly determined by mechanical facts. One age has the harpsichord, while another – benefiting from mechanical development – has the piano. In the twentieth century there became available the widest possible variety of colours.

In the nineteenth century the so-called 'symphony' orchestra grew to enormous size. In the twentieth century every country within the reach of Western classical music preserves a few large orchestras, whose main function is to perform music of the past. They thus serve a kind of museum function. At the same time, however, composers have continued to compose with this large opulent tonal palette in mind. Among the most notable twentieth-century works for large symphony orchestra are Stravinsky's *Rite of Spring* (1913), Bartók's *Concerto for Orchestra* (1943), and Olivier Messaien's (b. 1908) *Turangalîla*. Bartók's and Messaien's works were commissioned by the Koussevitzky Foundation and both were first played by the Boston Symphony Orchestra.

Composers have, however, generally been more interested in exploring new and often more subtle colour combinations. These have sometimes resulted from the necessity to be economical, sometimes from a wish to produce delicate and clear effects, sometimes from a combination of circumstances.

Neo-Baroque and neo-Classical principles have underpinned certain sonorities that are familiar in modern music, even in some popular music, where the organ (electronic) and the harpsichord are not unusual. These principles came into partnership with those relating to tonality, and in much of the music of Schoenberg and his successors, of whom the best known were Alban Berg (1885–1935) and Anton Webern (1887–1945), one is struck not only by the sparseness of the instrumentation but also the sparseness of the scores and the brevity of the pieces.

In reaction against former extravagances, modern art in some aspects was designed to be functional. Composers who followed the ideas of Schoenberg – one of the great teachers of composition – concerned themselves with the function of every sound in a musical texture. This resulted in the dissemination of new theories of composition, the most fashionable of which was the serial method. Very briefly, this was based on the development of musical meaning through the statement and restatement of a limited series of sounds and rhythms according to a theoretical scale of values that becomes increasingly complex. Masters of the most modern serial techniques are Pierre Boulez (b. 1925), who is also a brilliant conductor, and Karl-Heintz Stockhausen (b. 1928), both composers, however, have gone beyond this point in experimentation. Many young musicians who work under the influence of Boulez and Stockhausen also concern themselves with the relevance to music of mathematical and linguistic theories and the general matter of communication.

The character of music has been changed fundamentally by new techniques of communication. In the eighteenth century sheet music became widely available and, for the first time, a great body of music-lovers in many lands was able to acquire the scores (or, at least, the parts) of important works. Now, the recording of music enables people to build up their own libraries of music being performed.

Radio, television, and the film are the major agents of communication in the present time. The musician is employed to serve these media and out of his experience new forms and new techniques develop. Most obviously, perhaps, the composer has been affected by the whole science of electronics, and in the last twenty years electronically produced music has become an art in its own right. With electronic equipment the modern composer who prefers this medium, and recognizes that no intermediate 'interpreter' is required, is able to feel himself in direct touch with his audience.

By a paradox the composer of electronic music is often fulfilling the function of a composer of Classical times. He is the craftsman supplying what is wanted. In the eighteenth century the typical patron was a prince. In the twentieth century the typical patron is the communications industry, or the commercial organization requiring music either to support its advertising or else to enhance its prestige.

One line of musical thought grew out of the sense of revolt experienced by Arnold Schoenberg. In looking for new modes of musical expression, Schoenberg was registering a protest against a whole way of life. His successors may sometimes appear to have decided to withdraw themselves from the main stream of life altogether. The ultimate aims of musicians inspired solely by theoretical concepts may seem to be of doubtful value. The American musician John Cage has introduced theories of chance into musical expression so that those who are influenced by him appear to have to set no limits on what they do – or don't do. **Aleatoric** music is what turns up when it turns up: it is thought to be extremely advanced, but claims few adherents.

Aleatoric music, however, has within it another idea which at first glance is contrary to aleatoric principles, that of the freedom of the individual. The individual composer is the individual man. In the present age the individual often feels himself to be isolated, or alienated.

The theme of isolation runs through many modern compositions of an otherwise traditional character. Isolation is the theme of *Peter Grimes*, the most outstanding operatic work of Benjamin Britten (b. 1913).

Britten is an old-fashioned composer in that he views his function as a moral one. His music is created to express a social attitude and also to fulfil a social need. In the *War Requiem* he certainly succeeded in arousing many people in many countries to a new abhorrence of the divisive forces in the world and of the inhumanities of which man is capable. So far as social need is concerned, Britten has composed music of significance for the student in the schoolroom. In so doing he has helped to extend the vision of the many rather than of the few.

That music should be generally available is a principle dear to musicians. That it is a moral force is still accepted by many persons of authority in modern society. Those who are musical ask only that music be created and widely practised. The unmusical – including some of those who control the world's affairs – are anxious that only 'good' music shall be practised and created. And yet a proper definition of 'good' and 'bad' is wanting. There is no definition to be found.

In the meantime the same process goes on now as it did thousands of years ago. Men, women, and children sing and dance, and try to express themselves through an infinity of patterns of sound.

Glossary

Words in the Glossary have appeared in context in the main body of the book, where they are shown in bold type. These are basic terms of which both derivation and meaning are shown below. The large number of words of Latin and Greek origin shows the profound influence of these cultures on our own. There are, however, derivations from a large number of sources to show how many peoples have contributed to the development of musical thought.

Key to languages
Ar. – Arabic; arch. E. – archaic English; Fr. – French
Ger. – German; Gr. – Greek; It. – Italian; Lat. – Latin
Med. Lat. – medieval Latin; O.E. – old English; O.Fr. – old French
Pol. – Polish; Span. – Spanish; Welsh

Abstract art
Art which is not representational. By its nature music is necessarily the most abstract of the arts.
Lat. *abstractum* – removed from

Acoustics
The science of sound.   Gr. *akouein* – to hear

Aerophone
Wind instrument of any kind.
Gr. *aer* – air (atmosphere) *phone* – sound

Aesthetics
The general subject of beauty and the fundamentals of the fine arts.
Gr. *aesthesis* – perception through the senses

Aleatoric music
That which comes by chance, often as the result of everyone 'doing his own thing'.
Lat. *aleator* – a dice-player

Antiphon
Scriptural text set to *plainsong* melody with phrases sung by two alternating groups of singers. Hence antiphonal method of performance.
Gr. *anti* – opposite

Anthem
English Church composition, derived from antiphon and *motet*.

Aria
A song. The term is particularly applied to the A B A pattern popularized in the seventeenth–eighteenth century. (*See da capo.*)
It. *aira* – air (*also* wind)

Atonality
The principle underlying music not subject to the disciplines afforded by recognizable tonal centres. Much, if not most, western European and American music composed since 1945 has shown atonal features.
Gr. *a* – not *tonos* – tone (*see below*)

Aulos
Ancient wind instrument of reed, wood, bone, ivory, or metal, with a reed to activate sound.
Gr. *aulos* – often mistranslated as 'flute'

Baroque art
A dramatic type of expression often concerned with large-scale presentation, associated in the first place with the Catholic reaction to the Reformation (i.e. Counter-Reformation). Music from 1600 to 1750 is generally described as Baroque, while music of later time based on principles then in vogue is defined as *neo-baroque*.
Span. *barrueco* – a rough pearl; Gr. *neos* – new

Bel canto
A style of singing in which beauty of tone is the main aim. This style, which encouraged brilliance, dominated the Italian school of music.
It. *bel canto* – beautiful song

Bourrée
French dance in quick two time, beginning with weak upbeat. Often found in French ballets of the seventeenth century, and *suites*. Like other French dances of the period the bourrée became international and its spelling variable.

Cantata
An extended vocal piece, usually secular, with alternating *recitatives* and *arias*, of Italian origin.
A German development of cantata, often including choral movements based on *chorale*, is known as *Church Cantata*.
It. *cantata* – a work which is sung

Canzona
A choral piece of the sixteenth–seventeenth century usually in imitative *counterpoint*. Instrumental movements in similar style also described by this term.   It. *canzone* – song

Capellmeister (mod. *Kapellmeister*)
Originally applied to the functionary who was in

charge of the music of a court chapel, but later extended to cover director of secular music as well. Term reserved to German-speaking countries.

Ger. *Capelle* (mod. form, *Kapelle*) – chapel *Meister* – master

Carol
A work for one or more voices, often rooted in folk tradition, based on themes associated with Christmas, less frequently, Easter.

Fr. *carole* – a ring dance; It. *carolla* – a ring dance

Chamber music
Music for small groups of instrumentalists (sometimes with singers, e.g. *cantata*) primarily for private performance. Instrumental music from duets (two persons) to, say, octets (eight persons) and such vocal forms as *madrigal* qualify for this definition.

Works for *string quartet* (two violins, viola, violoncello) are generally thought to represent the most refined form of chamber music.

It. *camera* – room, chamber It. *camerata* – society

Chanson
A solo song or part-song of simple structure as developed in France and Flanders (*see aria* and *Lied*). Fr. *chanter* – to sing

Chorale
Hymn of the German Evangelical (Lutheran) Church. A more or less free treatment of chorale melodies in the seventeenth and eighteenth centuries by German organists resulted in the form of the chorale prelude.

The correct spelling of chorale in German is *Choral*. Gr. *chŏrŏs* – round dance (*see carol*) with vocal accompaniment. Singers became a select group, but term originally not restricted to singers

Chordophone
A stringed instrument.

Gr. *chorde* – string *phone* – sound

Classical
In general, 'classical' denotes balance and clarity in artistic expression.

Sonata form in its maturity appeared to enshrine the ideal of classical thought in music. For convenience, the period of Haydn-Mozart-Beethoven is termed the 'Classical era'.

Classical is loosely used in apposition to pop.

Lat. *classicus* – a citizen of high rank

Concerto
A piece of music for a number of performers rationalized in the late seventeenth century as *concerto grosso*. This was a work for soloists (the *concertino*) and a main group (of strings with *harpsichord*) known as the *concerto grosso*.

From the later eighteenth century concerto generally indicated a work in *sonata* form for solo instruments and orchestra. The classical concerto comprised three movements, the dance movement belonging to the *symphony* being omitted.

It. *con* – with (together) *certare* – to strive

Consort
A group of instruments in England in the sixteenth –seventeenth century. A 'whole' consort meant instruments of the same family (e.g. a consort of *recorders*); a 'broken' consort meant instruments of different families (e.g. as of *viols* and *recorders* and *sackbuts*). The term also applied to music composed for such combinations.

Consort and *concert* (Ger. *Konzert*, and *Konzertmeister* – Eng. 'leader of orchestra') derive from *concerto*.

Corno di caccia
Horns used for princely hunts in the eighteenth century were included in princely *orchestras* in order to remind princely audiences of the pleasures of blood sports. The instruments also served to keep such audiences awake. L. Mozart and J. F. Haydn and many others composed 'hunt' symphonies. Before long, however, the *corno* became house-trained and esteemed for the sake of its beautiful tone, which, nevertheless, continued to remind listeners of wooded landscapes and other rural delights.

It. *corno* – horn, *di caccia* – of the chase

Counterpoint
Music based on the principle of 'point against point', i.e. note, or melody, in contrast to and in combination with one or more others.

Lat. *contra* – against *punctus* – point

Da capo
When these words are encountered by a performer he is required to go back to the beginning of the piece he is performing. Having done this he waits until the word *Fine* (It. – end) appears, at which point his work is done. The *da capo* aria followed the pattern A B A. The final A section once was not written out, but repetition of A was supposed to include ornamentation improvised by the performer. Modern performances of *da capo* arias often include ornamentation thought up by *musicologists*. It. *da capo* – from the beginning

Decibel
One-tenth of a *bel*, a unit for measuring loudness derived from the name of Alexander Graham Bell (1847–1922), British-American vocal specialist and inventor of the telephone.

Dynamics
Dynamic markings (very few in number until the great explosion of terms in the *Romantic* period) are commonly termed 'expression marks'.

Gr. *dynamis* – power, strength

Eisteddfod
Festival of music, poetry, oratory, and so on in Wales, in which competitions take place. The tradition dates back to Bardic times, perhaps to the time of the Druids, and, although the tradition

was interrupted by English interference, the Welsh National Eisteddfod is probably the oldest, and certainly the most widely popular, musical festival in the Western world. An Eisteddfod is conducted in the Welsh language which the institution seeks to preserve.

Welsh – *eistedd* – to sit, hence *eisteddfod* – session

Electronics
Branch of physical science dealing with activity of electrons, as in photo-electric cells, vacuum tubes, etc. Much of modern life is controlled by electronics. Sound created by electronic means is the material out of which *electronic music* is formed.

The 'electronic organ' has electronic oscillators as sound generators, and often imitates the 'natural' tone of organ-pipes.

Gr. *electron* – gleaming metallic substance

Fantasia
A piece, or a section of a piece, in which fancy may be thought to have free rein. Some fantasias are independent, others are forms of *variations* on a given theme.   It. *fantasia* – fancy, imagination

Frottola
Italian song for several voices, often of a distinctively popular character, that was among the forerunners of the *madrigal*.   It. *frotta* – crowd

Fugue
A contrapuntal movement in which one subject, or melodic idea, is stated in one part and then rather strictly imitated in the others. Fugal textures frequently show much ingenuity in design.

It. *fuga* – flight

Gavotte
French quick dance in four time, beginning on third beat, often found in a *suite* (see *bourrée*).

Gewandhaus
Ancient Cloth Hall in Leipzig where concerts were held. The title has remained so that the leading orchestra in Leipzig is still known as the Gewandhaus Orchestra.

Ger. *Gewand* – garment, *Haus* – house

Gothic
Style of architecture distinguished by use of pointed arches that succeeded the *Romanesque*. The style was rudely termed Gothic during the *Renaissance* period by scholars who did not like it and could not think what else to call it. The Goths were a rough Germanic tribe, who had nothing to do with architectural styles.

Gregorian chant
The traditional form of melody for the liturgy of the Roman Catholic Church since the time of Pope Gregory I (about 540–604), who reorganized the music of the Church.

Harmonic
One of a series of sounds subsidiary to the principal sound created by a vibrating body. Such sounds, also known as 'overtones', are found to have a regular, mathematical relationship with one another and with their fundamental (principal sound).

Harmony
The art and science of combining separate musical sounds into clusters (chords) which have significance in themselves and in relation to one another. The principles of traditional Western harmony evolved from the laws of acoustics.

Gr. *harmonia* – covenant, decree, *hence* concord

Harpsichord
A keyboard instrument, sometimes with more than one manual (keyboard), in which sound is produced by the plucking of strings by 'quills'. The harpsichord was an important factor in Baroque music and is much in vogue at the present time, and not only for the performance of old music.

The Italian term *clavicembalo* (or *cembalo*) and the French *clavecin* (Lat. *clavis* – key) are frequently to be met with.

O.E. *hearpe* – harp Gr. *chorde* – string (of a lyre)

Laudi spirituali
It. *lauda* – hymn of praise *spirituale* – spiritual

Idiophone
Object, or instrument, that produces musical sound when struck. Members of the percussion group are basically idiophone instruments.

Gr. *idios* – own *phone* – sound

Intonation
In regard to speech, the rise and fall of pitch. Musically – in tune. When a player or singer is off pitch the intonation is said to be faulty.

Med. Lat. *intonare* – to intone

Libretto
Text of opera, oratorio, cantata, or any other extended work for voices with (or very occasionally without) instruments.

It. *libro* – book *libretto* – little book

Lied
Song, applying particularly to German song of the *Romantic* period.

Ger. *Lied* – song (*see aria, chanson*)

Lute
Stringed instrument made in many different forms, characterized by a deep body and long, fretted finger-board, and popular in the sixteenth–seventeenth century.

Ar. *al ʿud* – instrument similar to lute

Lydian mode
A *mode* so called in the Middle Ages under the impression that it was related to a type of mode originating in pre-Christian times in Lydia (Greece).

Lyric
Poem originally to be chanted or sung to accompaniment of the lyre; later, any poem with musical

feeling, or that kind of feeling in general. Hence a *Lyric Suite* (Grieg).

Gr. *lyra* – lyre (of seven strings)

Madrigal
A part-song, particularly of the sixteenth–seventeenth century, characterized by contrapuntal textures and frequent delight in word-painting. Madrigal flourished especially in Italy and Britain.

It. *madrigale* (origin uncertain)

Major
Term used to describe particular melodic intervals, of which the major third (e.g. *doh–me*) is the most important, and harmonies and *scales* dominated by the major third. The opposite of major is *minor*, and the development of Baroque and Classical music was determined largely by the contrast between major and minor tonalities.

Lat. *major* – larger

Mass
Principal service of Roman Catholic liturgy, but the term is also used by some Episcopalians and by Lutherans. Parts of the Mass which remain constant (Kyrie, Gloria, Credo, Sanctus, Benedictus, Agnus Dei) are frequently set to music and the result is also called a Mass. A Mass for the Dead is a Requiem Mass. The word is derived from the final part of the liturgy.

Lat. *Ite missa est* – Go, it is ended

Mazurka
Traditional Polish dance in three time with accents on weak beats. The Mazury region of Poland was in the province of Mazowsze (in which Warsaw lies); hence Chopin sometimes described himself as an 'old Mazur'. The native dance was also known as a *Mazur*. The stylized dance took the diminutive of *Mazur – Mazurek*.

Pol. *Mazurek – Mazurka* (feminine form)

Membranophone
Instrument with stretched skin usually of the drum family (but *see mirliton*).

Lat. *membrana* – skin Gr. *phone* – sound

Minnesinger
German equivalent of *troubadour*.

Ger. *Minne* – love *singen* – to sing

Minor
Lah–doh provides an example of a minor third interval. The *scale* based on *lah* was the basis of minor tonality (*see also major*).

Lat. *minor* – smaller

Minuet
French dance in three time popular in the seventeenth and eighteenth centuries. Often found in early ballets, suites, overtures, and symphonies.

Fr. *menu* – small

Mirliton
A pipe closed by a skin. Fr. *mirliton* – reed-pipe

Mode
A sequence of notes arranged as in a *scale* but primarily relating to medieval music, certain modes having been regularized by Pope Gregory I.

Lat. *modus* – measure, *also* melody, rhythm

Monochord
A single string stretched over a resonator, used for theoretical purposes in the Middle Ages.

Gr. *monos* – alone *chorde* – string

Motet
Composition for voices initially to Latin Biblical text sung during a service but not obligatory.

Fr. *mot* – word

Music-drama
The arts of music and drama together, ideally where neither is more important than the other. Richard Wagner preferred this term – which had also been used in earlier times – to *opera*. The modern opera-goer makes no distinction between the two, but says he is going to the opera even when he is going to a music-drama.

Musicology
Studies relating to the history and general theory of music and sometimes to problems of performance comprise the main body of musicology. A practitioner in the field of musicology is known as a 'musicologist'. Gr. *Mousike* – any art presided over by a Muse and then music in particular, *logos* – reason

Neume
A sign used in manuscript copies of Gregorian music to indicate pitch. Neumatic *notation* was also used for troubadour songs and early *polyphony*. Staff notation developed from neumatic notation.

Gr. *pneuma* – breath

Notation
Any method for giving visual form to music so that the music can be recreated in performance. Neumatic notation developed into staff notation which is the most familiar method of writing music down. But systems based on alphabetical names and on the division of a string have proved serviceable. These systems are known as 'tablatures'.

Lat. *nota* – a mark

Opera
A presentation of a plot on a stage by means of singing, acting, and scenic devices. Formerly there were two main types, *opera seria* (serious opera) and *opera buffa* (comic opera) (*see music-drama*). Lat. *opus* – work *opera* (*plural*) – trouble, exertion It. *opera* – work

Oratorio
Musico-dramatic work of religious character similar to opera in form but without action.

It. *oratorio* – a church (chapel) established for presentation of popular services during Counter-Reformation

Orchestra

In the seventeenth-century opera-house instrumental musicians were placed where in ancient Greek theatre the dancers had been stationed, and the Greek word was taken over to define not only the place but the players. When groups of instrumentalists functioned independently of the opera-house they were still described as members of an orchestra. Gr. *orchestra* – a place for dancing in classical Greek theatre

Overtone

See harmonic

Passacaglia

Variations on a theme in three time based on a Spanish dance. The theme is first stated in bass part and for the most part kept in the bass. The passacaglia form was popular in the Baroque era.
Span. *pasar* – to walk, *calle* – street

Passion

The events of the Passion of Christ as described in the Bible furnished the basis of important music-liturgical works from the Middle Ages on. Such works were described as 'passions'.
Gr. *pascō* – I suffer; Lat. *passus sum* – I suffered

Pentatonic scale

Five-note group (d, r, f, s, l in *sol-fa* system) fundamental to most folk-song; brought back into art music during later stages of *Romantic* period.
Gr. *penta* – five, *tonos* – a tone

Percussion

See idiophone. Percussion instruments, however, may be tuned as well as untuned, as in the case of xylophones, bells, vibraphones, for instance.
Lat. *percutio* – I strike

Pibcorn (Pibgorn)

A wind instrument, of wood or bone, with reed, used by Welsh people (and others) in early times.
Corruption of *pipe* and *horn*

Plainsong

See *Gregorian* chant which was also described as plainsong. Lat. *cantus* – song, *planus* – level

Polonaise

Polish national dance – *Polonez* – of festive character in three time, popularized especially by F. Chopin. Fr. *polonaise* – Polish (feminine form)

Polyphony

Music, more often for voices, in many parts and contrapuntal. Gr. *pollus* – many, *phone* – sound

Portatif

A small movable organ of medieval period, useful for processions. Fr. *porter* – to carry

Positif

An organ that, in contrast to the portatif, remained in one place. Fr. *positif* – positive

Prelude

Usually an introductory movement, although some pieces entitled prelude are independent and self-sufficient (*see Chorale*). A prelude frequently prefaced a fugue. Lat. *prae* – before *ludere* – to play

Programme music

Music with a descriptive purpose, composed according to a 'programme' set by a story or a picture. Programme music was particularly popular during the Romantic era.
Gr. *pro* – before, *gramma* – what is written

Psaltery

A triangular stringed instrument played with fingers or plectrum, popular in Middle Ages.
Gr. *psallo* – I play on strings . . .
Gr. *psalmos* – a song accompanied by strings

Recitative

Setting of words to music in which speech rhythms are allowed to prevail. In Baroque and Classical music recitative was the usual lead-in to *aria*.
It. *recitativo*

Recorder

Flute with 'fipple' mouthpiece used up to the eighteenth century, when it was replaced by the 'German' or transverse flute, and revived in the twentieth century.
arch. E. *to record* – to sing like a bird

Regal

A portable organ with reed-pipes invented in the fifteenth century. Lat. *regalis* – royal

Renaissance

The movement, starting in the fourteenth century and continuing until its full effects were felt in the sixteenth century, which was a reaction against the confining ideas of the Middle Ages. This was helped by a re-examination of the works of the writers, artists, and philosophers of classical Greece and Rome. Fr. *renaître* – to be born again

Resonance

This occurs when the vibrations from one body are taken up by another, thus resonators are used to give body to, or amplify, sound.
Lat. *resonare* – to sound again, to echo

Rhythm

The pattern of stresses that vitalizes the time element in musical creation. The word is extended to cover, for example, patterns in the visual arts.
Gr. *rhythmos* – measured motion, form, proportion, method

Ricercare

Instrumental movement patterned after vocal contrapuntal piece, and predecessor of *fugue*.
It. *ricercare* – to inquire, to search

Rococo

A florid style in art in the eighteenth century characterized by naturalistic flower and shell ornamentation and developed particularly in France and Germany.
It. *rocaille* – pebble, rock-work

Romanesque
Architectural style dominated by the round arch established in Europe by the Romans and continued until the *Gothic* style evolved in the twelfth century.

Rondo
A musical dance and song form derived from the poetic form of *rondeau* (A B A C A D A, etc.). The rondo, as designed in the Classical period, absorbed facets of sonata form and the concluding movement of a classical work in sonata style was frequently an enlarged rondo.   Fr. *rond* – round

Sackbut
Early form of the trombone.
                O.Fr. *sacqueboute* – pull-push

Sarabande
French-Spanish dance in slow three time that may have originated in Mexico. Often found in *suite*.

Scale
A series of sounds progressively set out and representing the basic sounds of the musical idiom of a particular period. Between about 1600 and about 1900 European music was controlled by the major and minor scales.   Lat. *scala* – ladder

Scherzo
A quick, dance-like, movement used in symphony in place of the earlier minuet. In the seventeenth century certain lighthearted part-songs were called *scherzi musicali*.   It. *Scherzo* – fun, joke

Semitone
The smallest interval hitherto used in Western-style music; e.g. the progression *te–doh*.
                Lat. *semi* – half

Singspiel
A play with songs in popular style in German countries, seen as an antidote to Italian opera. *Singspiel* and opera came together to provide a basis for Romantic opera and music-drama.
            Ger. *singen* – to sing, *spielen* – to play

Sol-fa
A system whereby sounds in a scale were denoted by syllables: (*ut*)=*do re mi fa soh la* (*si*)=*te doh*. The principle, in use in the twelfth century, was modified and widely applied by John Curwen (1816–80). Since the syllables were related to the tonic of each key the system became known by its present name.

Sonata
In the sixteenth and seventeenth centuries loosely applied to instrumental pieces. Towards the end of the seventeenth century the *sonata da chiesa* (Church sonata) and the *sonata da camera* (chamber sonata) were regularized. The former consisted of slow, fast, slow, fast movements, the latter of dances prefaced by an introduction. In the course of the eighteenth century the complex form of Introduction, Exposition (A and B themes),

Development (of previous material), Recapitulation set around a logical scheme of *tonalities* emerged. This reached maturity during the Classical era. A complete sonata (or similar work) comprised first movement (quick), second movement (slow and lyrical), minuet (replaced by *scherzo*), rondo.

String quartet
See Chamber music

Suite
A group of contrasting pieces (formerly dances) linked together sometimes by *tonality*, sometimes by subject.   Fr. *suite* – retinue, succession

Symphonic poem
A one-movement work of symphonic dimensions and constructed according to symphonic structural principles, but programmatic in character.

Symphony
In the seventeenth century 'symphony' indicated merely a piece of music for instruments. For a time symphony was synonymous with overture. The practice of playing symphonies for operas as independent items stimulated the composition of symphonies for concert use. In the Classical period the symphony, designed according to sonata-form principles, became the focal point of musical attention.   Gr. *syn* – with *phone* – sound

Timbre
Distinctive quality of any sound.
            Fr. *timbre* – bell, sound, tone character

Toccata
A fast, brilliant piece, initially for keyboard.
                It. *toccare* – to touch

Tonality
The quality distinguishing music constructed according to principles based on a system of related tonal centres. In general this is understood as the major and minor key system.
                Gr. *tonos* – a chord, a sinew, a strain,
                a tone (of the voice)

Tone
In contrast to semitone, sometimes described as 'whole-tone', an interval containing two semitones; e.g. *doh-re* (*see whole-tone scale*).

Troubadour
A poet-musician, usually of the ruling class, in southern France in the Middle Ages.
 O.Fr. *trobador* – a 'searcher', i.e. a poet-musician
        Fr. *trouver* – to find

Trouvère
French minstrel, whose art was related to that of the troubadour; the trouvère, however, was a professional.

Variation
Composing (or extemporizing) variations on a given theme is one of the most frequent forms of creative musical exercise. Variations may consist of

decorations or, more ambitiously, commentaries on various aspects of a theme.

Viol
This term covers the family of bowed stringed instruments that preceded that of the violin. Much seventeenth-century *chamber music* was for consorts of viols.

O.Fr. *vielle* – fiddle; O.E. *fithele* – fiddle

Virginals (pair of)
Small keyboard instrument with strings activated by mechanism similar to that of harpsichord. Generally referred to as 'pair of virginals'. English composers of sixteenth–seventeenth century composed much music for this instrument.

Origin doubtful; possibly attributable to the fact that the virginals sounded 'lady-like', or to the compulsion on girls of good family to learn to play it.

Whole-tone scale
The *major* scale of seven intervals comprises five tones and two half- or semitones. The whole-tone scale of six intervals consists only of whole tones.

Xylophone
A row of wooden bars of differing pitch played by hammers. Xylophones of one sort or another are used in tribal music. A more scientifically constructed form of xylophone is to be found in the percussion department of a symphony orchestra.

Gr. *xylon* – wood, *phone* – sound

Acknowledgements

The author and publishers wish to thank copyright owners for the use of the illustrations listed below:

Ashmolean Museum, Oxford, for: 9
Austrian National Library, Picture Collection, for: 15
Boston Public Library, for: 65, 69
British Museum, for: 18, 19, 22, 34, 36, 37, 52, 54, 62, 64
Camera Press Ltd., for: 57
Carillon Museum, Mechlen, for: 63
City Library, Birmingham, for: 2
Detroit Institute of Arts, for: 16
Deutscher Verlag für Musik, Leipzig, for: 12, 55
Dresden Picture Gallery, for: 56
E.M.I., The Gramophone Co. Ltd., for: 14, 66
Eisenstadt Town Archives, for: 44, 45
The Frick Collection, New York, for: 38
German National Museum, Nürnberg, for: 35
Grosvenor Museum, Chester, for: 27
Zbignien Grzybowski, for: 71
Handel Museum, Halle/Saale, for: 30, 31, 51, 58
Illustrated London News, for: 61
Jena University Library, for: 33
Kenya Information Services, for: 4, 5
Jutta Landgraf, for: 67, 68, 74, 75
Liverpool City Library, for: 21
Robert Morley & Co. Ltd., for: 60
National Gallery, London, for: 24, 25, 26
National Museum of Wales, Welsh Folk Museum, for: 7, 29, 59
National Széchényi Library, Budapest, for: title-page
New York Public Library, for: 17
Newcastle upon Tyne City Library, for: 53
Oberlin College, Ohio, for: 76
Pergamon Museum, Berlin, for: 10
Royal Museum of Fine Arts, Antwerp, for: 23
State Collection of the Arts, Munich, for: 49, 50
State Ethnological Museum, Munich, for: 8
Tate Gallery, London, for: 40
Victoria and Albert Museum, London, for: 28
Walters Art Gallery, Baltimore, for: 6

Index

Page numbers shown below in *italics* refer to illustrations

Printed in Great Britain by Jarrold & Sons Limited, Norwich